Hamlyn all-colour paperbacks

# Birdwatching

David S

illust
John

**Hamlyn**
London · New York · Sydney · Toronto

# FOREWORD

Birdwatching is one of those hobbies which may be enjoyed by everyone, the young, the old, the active and the housebound, whether in town or country. The ways in which we can participate are legion, with many aspects and choices for the observer. There are those who become so involved that it becomes a full-time occupation, though loses none of its excitement because of this. By contrast, there are others who hardly think of themselves as birdwatchers, simply people content to obtain their pleasure in a casual way. It is for these, and to those whose interest in this, most appealing of natural history hobbies, is just awakening, that this book is written.

I hope in this slim volume to cover all aspects of birdwatching, though naturally the emphasis will be a personal one. My intention is to show you the variety and excitement to be obtained through watching birds, and at the same time, how you can contribute to the hobby, perhaps by feeding birds in the garden or by providing a nestbox, or on a larger scale, by participating in a national survey. In this way even greater pleasure will accrue.

Birdwatching should not be looked at in isolation. To ensure we always have birds to watch, common as well as rare, we must care about their environment and the changes that are taking place in it. The greater knowledge we have of each bird's requirements, the better our position in this crowded island will be when decisions are taken regarding changes in land use. If more people take up bird-watching after reading this book then it will have served its purpose in assisting with the correct management of our wild birds.          D.S.

*The tally list on page 63 and the nest record card on page 91 are reproduced by courtesy of the British Trust for Ornithology.*

Published by The Hamlyn Publishing Group Limited
London · New York · Sydney · Toronto
Astronaut House, Feltham, Middlesex, England

Copyright © The Hamlyn Publishing Group Limited 1975
ISBN 0 600 31341 7

Phototypeset by Filmtype Services Limited, Scarborough, England
Colour separations by Metric Reproductions Limited, Chelmsford, England
Printed in Spain by Mateu Cromo, Madrid

# CONTENTS

# INTRODUCTION

Some 8,600 species of birds are alive at the present time, distributed through all parts of the world from high polar regions to the tropics, from arid deserts to the ocean centres. The highest concentration of species is found in South America where no less than 3,500 have been described; the European avifauna is not nearly so rich, only about 570 species occurring. Some, like the Booted Eagle *Hieraaetus pennatus* and Rock Nuthatch *Sitta neumayer,* have a restricted range, not extending north to Great Britain where only 475 species have been recorded, though this list slowly grows with almost annual additions.

Many of the 475 are rare vagrants to Britain, like the Killdeer *Charadrius vociferus* which has accidentally crossed the Atlantic from North America on less than twenty occasions, or the Eye-browed Thrush *Turdus obscurus* from eastern Asia, observed only during the autumn of 1964 when three individuals were noted. Delete such species from the British list and our total is reduced to about 270. These are birds which either breed in Great Britain, regularly visit us on spring or autumn migration, like the Little Stint *Calidris minuta*, or winter here, like the Whooper Swan *Cygnus cygnus*. An industrious birdwatcher able to travel extensively might reasonably expect to see many of these in the course of a year.

For most of us birdwatching is restricted to weekends near home and the annual holiday when we may wander further afield. Nevertheless, many interesting and colourful species can be encountered without great efforts and vast travelling expenses. There are, of course, regional differences; a birdwatcher on the coast has greater opportunities than someone inland. Similarly, the south-east has more species than western and northern Britain, though these regions have birds, like the Ptarmigan *Lagopus mutus* and Dipper *Cinclus cinclus,* rarely, if ever, met in the former area. Wherever we live there are always birds to watch and discoveries about them to be made. The Chaffinch *Fringilla coelebs* was once described as 'too common to be well known'; the same can be said for many other species

Some of the interesting and colourful species of birds to be seen near our homes.

Wood Pigeon

House Martin

Bullfinch

Blue Tit

House Sparrow

Song Thrush

which live close to our homes and provide us with so much pleasure.

Despite a bustling human population continually requiring more space for its many activities, we have in Great Britain a wide range of habitats. On the other hand, our size and position in relation to the rest of Europe exclude certain habitats. For instance, our mountain ranges are of modest altitude, exceeding 4,000 feet (1,200 metres) only in Scotland. Neither do we have the immense marshland and delta areas which exist at the mouths of some great European rivers.

Not one of our habitats has escaped man's attention since he first commenced forest clearance in Neolithic times (4,000 B.C.). Felling, replanting, drainage, agriculture, housing, industry and leisure pursuits have all had their affects, in some cases leading to a loss of habitat, in others a gain. We have lost virtually all our large marshlands and reedbeds, but on the other hand, some aquatic species have been able to take advantage of new reservoirs and the excavation of gravel pits. The coastlines of Great Britain, particularly in the north and

west, provide ideal breeding grounds for multitudes of sea-birds; indeed for some it is their North Atlantic stronghold. Estuarine areas are also important, especially in winter, for waders and wildfowl.

These are all major habitats, but it is usually possible to encounter a variety of areas in which to watch birds within a short distance of your home. Gardens are always full of interest and easily observed from the house. Reservoirs or lakes are found close to most towns, while in the country there

Bearded Reedlings (*left*) and Dartford Warblers (*below left*) are confined to reedbed and heath habitats respectively, whereas the Carrion Crow (*below*) occurs anywhere.

are farm ponds. Woodland in the form of shelter-belts, even in large churchyards, can often prove as interesting as huge plantations and should not be neglected.

Some birds are catholic in their requirements, such as the Carrion Crow *Corvus corone*, occurring virtually everywhere. Many woodland species have been able to adapt to change and are now as frequent in our shrubberies as in a copse. Others, like the House Martin *Delichon urbica*, have also taken advantage of man. A few unable to adapt, like the Bearded Reedling *Panurus biarmicus* and Dartford Warbler *Sylvia undata* have diminished in numbers to a few restricted localities.

7

Birds are watched by more people than any other class of plants or animals. To a few – nature reserve wardens, scientists from organizations like the Natural Environment Research Council and the British Trust for Ornithology, and students carrying out postgraduate research – it may be a full-time job. For many it is an absorbing hobby, involving them in long hours of careful observation. However, to the vast majority birdwatching is a pleasurable leisure pastime, carried out to a variable degree of intensity. Birds can be watched from the windows of our homes and as we travel to our place of employment; indeed wherever we are or whatever we are doing, there will be birds in the vicinity.

What makes birds so attractive? Undoubtedly it is the ease with which many species can be seen. Their conspicuous habits, bright colours, and for part of the year at least their loud and pleasurable songs, all bring them easily to our attention.

Many birds are brightly coloured. Look no further than the garden and this can be seen quite clearly. The Great Tit *Parus major*, Robin *Erithacus rubecula* and Bullfinch *Pyrrhula pyrrhula*, are all excellent examples. In some, like the two former species, the sexes are similar; in others, like the Bullfinch, there may be differences and in the majority of these the females are duller.

With or without bright colours birds draw our attention by their songs and call notes. These, once learnt by an observer, provide sure clues to identification even when the bird is not visible. For instance, how many people see the first Cuckoo *Cuculus canorus*, or even any Cuckoo; yet this bird's call note, perhaps the most distinctive of all, is a sure guide to the bird's presence. Birds flying overhead may often be safely identified only by their call notes, an excellent means when mixed flocks of finches are on passage.

Compare birds with some other classes of animals and plants. Flowering plants are in most cases also conspicuous and brightly coloured, though only for part of the year, being greatly reduced in size or not visible during the winter months. Our mammal fauna is small and most of its members have inconspicuous habits making observation difficult. Butterflies are some of the most brightly coloured and easily identifiable of insects, though the field activities of a lepidop-

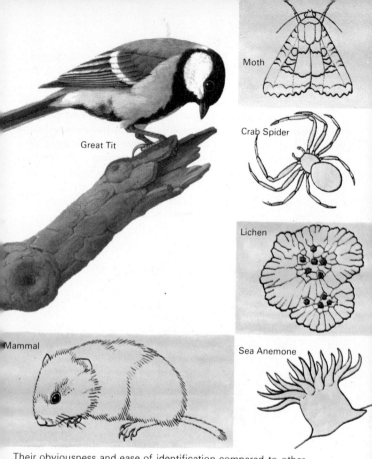

Great Tit

Moth

Crab Spider

Lichen

Mammal

Sea Anemone

Their obviousness and ease of identification compared to other classes of animals and plants help explain the popularity of birds.

terist are restricted to a few summer months. As we proceed further into the invertebrate legions, small size, difficulty of viewing and acute identification problems, often requiring complex keys and the use of a lens or binocular microscope, rule out all but the specialist. Small wonder that by contrast birds, with their large size, bright colours, conspicuous nature and year-long presence, hold pride of place in most people's attention.

9

# INTRODUCING THE BIRD

In 1861 a fossil was found in a Bavarian slate quarry which would have been classified as a reptile but for the fact that it had the distinct imprint of wings and feathers. Named *Archaeopteryx*, meaning 'ancient wing', it dates from the Upper Jurassic period, a warm, moist age some 160 million years ago. Although earlier birds or 'sub-birds' undoubtedly existed none has yet been found; *Archaeopteryx*, however, provides a very clear indication of the former close connection with reptiles. Despite the feathers its skeleton was still very much that of a

The lizard-like head and skeleton and wing claws of the fossil *Archaeopteryx* clearly indicate its reptilian ancestry.

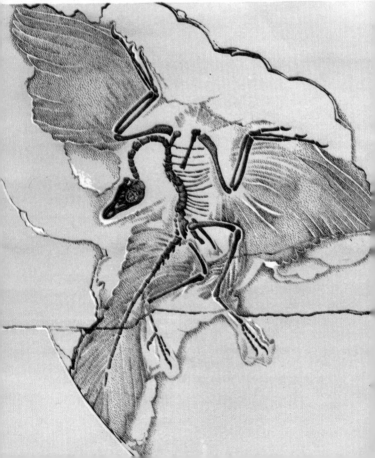

reptile with nearly solid bones, a long bony tail, strong jaws and teeth. A little larger than a Jackdaw *Corvus monedula*, it was not capable of prolonged flight, but probably flapped rather unsteadily about, its claws being particularly useful to grasp foliage and branches when landing.

Well over 160 million years have elapsed since birds branched away from their original reptilian stock, but they have nevertheless retained some of its characteristics. One of the most obvious is that both reptiles and birds lay large eggs with thick shells, and a high proportion of yolk. The scales of reptiles and birds are of a very similar structure, but in birds are confined to the feet and lower leg.

We are indeed lucky to have information concerning *Archaeopteryx*, only three specimens and a single feather having been found, for the avian fossil record is very incomplete when compared to other vertebrates and some invertebrates. Birds are generally small and fragile and their bodies easily destroyed so that few fossils are discovered. Most belong to aquatic species whose bodies are soon covered by silt and thus preserved after sinking to the bottoms of lakes or slow-running rivers. Terrestrial species are much more likely to be eaten by scavengers and their bones scattered, so that our records of these are more sparse.

The next fossil birds to be found date from the Cretaceous period, some thirty million years younger than *Archaeopteryx*. During the intervening period birds had evidently become well established; indeed one – *Hesperornis* – had become so adapted for an aquatic environment that it had lost the powers of flight. During the Eocene period (sixty to forty million years ago) the first representatives of modern families occur, including herons, geese, rails, partridges, pheasants and swifts. This may be called the Age of Birds, though not until the Pliocene period (thirteen to two million years ago) did species which exist today emerge.

Only about 800 bird species have been described from the fossil record; however, it has been estimated that since *Archaeopteryx* no less than 1,634,000 species have arisen, those living today forming little more than one half of one per cent of this total. The rest have gone, some without trace. while the others, able to adapt to a changing world, have evolved into one or more new species. This is a continuous process and one which can be seen even within the confines of Great Britain at the present time.

The population of a bird at one end of its breeding range often differs in size, sometimes colour, from that perhaps several thousand miles distant, while birds in between will exhibit intermediate stages. This geographic variation may eventually be taken a stage further when populations of the same species become separated, perhaps by changes in climate or isolation on islands. Differences will gradually become more pronounced and ecological requirements will alter.

The Wren *Troglodytes troglodytes* shows this quite clearly in north-western Europe where it occurs as a number of races or subspecies. Those breeding throughout much of Great Britain, the Shetlands and Iceland are darker than those on the continent of Europe, a change typical of birds inhabiting mild, moist regions. By contrast, the Wrens of Fair Isle, St Kilda and the Faeroes are greyer and much more barred, differences considered to be the result of living on high, cliff-bound islands. Over the course of thousands of years these island races may further separate from their original mainland stock, so that eventually new species will have evolved.

Most scientific names of birds are based on Latin or Greek though sometimes latinized words from other languages may be used. In the case of the St Kilda Wren *Troglodytes troglodytes hirtensis* the first, or generic name is from the Greek meaning hole frequenter, the second or species name in this wren is the same, while the third or subspecies name is from the Gaelic name for Hirta, the main St Kilda island.

Birds are classified by what is known of their relationship with other species and families; thus, Wrens are close to the tits, nuthatches and creepers; look in any bird book and you will find all three occur together. On this basis birds can be listed, or catalogued, proceeding from primitive species upwards. Ornithologists never quite agree as to the precise order, so slight differences in bird lists do occur.

Distribution of the races or subspecies of the Wren throughout north-west Europe.

Mainland Wren

Hebridean Wren

St Kilda Wren

Shetland Wren

Fair Isle Wren

Faeroes Wren

Norwegian Wren

Iceland Wren

Mainland Wren

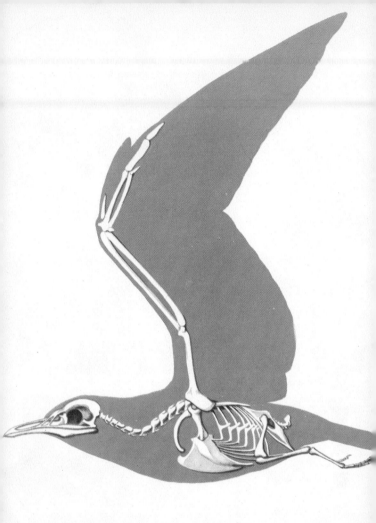

Look at the birds in your garden and although the different species which you see vary considerably in many respects – colour, size, song – their basic design revolves around the necessity to keep warm and to fly. All birds have feathers yet no other animal has them. Feathers occur as a number of different types each serving a particular purpose, such as the down feathers which lie close to the body and prevent heat loss, or the vane feathers giving the bird its outward shape. Each feather is a complex structure of a beauty and intricacy that can only be fully appreciated when viewed with the aid of a microscope. The barbs extending outwards from the main shaft have innumerable side branches – barbules – which in turn have equally innumerable barbicels, many of which are hooked. All lock together, trapping air in tiny cavities, or providing a flight surface to push against the air.

In general, most birds have slightly higher body temperatures than mammals, normally about 40°C compared to 37°C in man. Feathers act as a valuable insulating material, maintaining the high body temperature in cold weather when birds will fluff out their feathers so that more air can be trapped, and preventing overheating in warm conditions. Air remains among the feathers of aquatic birds when they dive and again keeps the birds warm; indeed large numbers are able to live in the food-rich polar seas. Birds carry more feathers in winter than in summer; the House Sparrow *Passer domesticus* having about 3,600 during the cold months, but only about 3,000 during the warmer part of the year.

The avian skeleton is highly adapted for flight, with hollow bones which not only provide great strength but also reduce body weight. The rib case and part of the backbone have become rigid with some bones fused. In addition to its lungs which are comparatively small, birds have numerous air sacs extending throughout the body and to many bones, so are thus able to use the air they breathe most efficiently. A keel has developed on the breast bone to which the huge pectoral (flight) muscles are attached. These may comprise up to 25 per cent of the body weight compared to a mere 1 per cent in man.

The skeleton of a gull shown against its outline in flight. The red section of this wing covert (*left*) is shown magnified to reveal the intricate interlocking structure of the barbules and barbicels.

For successful breeding birds must have an area around the nest undisturbed by other members of the same species. This is usually described as the territory, the simplest definition of which is 'any defended area'. There is a great variety of territories; some may be held by males, others by females, others by the pair. Most are retained only for the breeding season, but a few resident species maintain a territory throughout the year. In some cases the territory is no more than the nest itself, as in highly colonial species, such as the Gannet *Sula bassana*. By contrast, members of the tit family have territories extending up to 4 acres (1.6 hectares), while a larger species like the Tawny Owl *Strix aluco* requires up to 30 acres (12 hectares). The shape of a territory, other than the simplest forms, is dependent on the habitat, and the pressures exerted by neighbouring pairs of the same species. Some may be definitely linear; for instance, those of river bank birds, such as the Dipper, or hedgerow birds, such as the Yellowhammer *Emberiza citrinella*.

Most breeding territories are established by the male. In migrant birds these usually arrive first, so that courtship can commence in the territories without delay once the females appear. Males usually have a number of prominent song positions within the territory. By locating these, and by noting where encounters take place with adjacent males, it is usually possible to establish the size and shape of a territory without too much difficulty.

Instead of singing from a fixed position some species may engage in song flights; perhaps the best known of these is the Skylark *Alauda arvensis*. A few produce sounds mechanically, like the drumming of the Great Spotted Woodpecker *Dendrocopos major* which rapidly taps a dead branch. It may do this for as many as 500 times a day during courtship. The Common Snipe *Gallinago gallinago* makes a drumming sound in flight as it dives about the sky with the outer tail feathers spread, so causing a loud vibrating sound. Lapwings *Vanellus vanellus* plunge-flight over their nesting grounds, the wings

Robin from blue territory gives threat display and sings a warning to brown territory Robin which has entered his territory. Other territories (coloured) can be seen behind the cottage.

aggressive posture

submission

retreating male

Some examples of Blackbird displays you can observe in urban situations.

producing a humming throb as the birds tilt from side to side.

Some of the most spectacular of bird displays are performed by birds not holding a normal territory. The males of both the Black Grouse *Lyrurus tetrix* and Ruff *Philomachus pugnax* gather at traditional sites where each will hold a small patch of ground, the Black Grouse displaying its spectacular tail feathers, the Ruff its head and neck adornments. Females attracted to the area select a mate and pairing takes place, after which they move away to engage in nest building, incubation and the rearing of chicks, entirely alone. Some males may mate with several females, others not at all.

Bird displays as interesting, if not quite as dramatic, can be observed about our homes. The Robin pugnaciously defends its territory, driving off all other Robins. Should a female approach an unmated male his reaction is the same, but instead of retreating as intruders do, she will persistently fly right up to crouch submissively in front of him, occasionally engaging in song. This behaviour may continue for several hours before the male commences to follow her about the territory, and so the pair is formed.

In woodland Blackbirds *Turdus merula* are shy; usually all one sees are the birds moving off to the accompaniment of loud

aggressive posture

soliciting female

alarm calls. By contrast they become surprisingly unafraid in urban situations, and are thus an ideal species to watch for courtship displays. These are seen mainly during February and March. The male partially raises its crown feathers, compresses the neck feathers but fluffs out those on the body, particularly near the rump; at the same time the tail is fanned and dropped. Maintaining this posture it moves around the female, bowing from time to time and uttering what has been described as a low 'strangled song'.

Such displays as these are a most noticeable and necessary part of pair formation, a prelude to nest building, copulation and egg-laying. In many species the female takes the greater share of nest building though the male often assists. Only the female Rook *Corvus frugilegus* builds, though the male brings nest materials. The male Starling *Sturnus vulgaris* builds the nest foundation which the female lines with softer materials. The male Wren builds several 'cock's nests' within its territory, one of which will be selected and lined by the female ready for egg laying. Another of these nests may be used for a second brood.

Birds spend a great deal of their time feeding or searching for food; this is specially true during the winter months when

Wader bills show adaptations for different styles of feeding in wetland habitat.

Curlew

Black-tailed Godwit

Lapwing

Oystercatcher

Avocet

Dunlin

20

the weather is cooler and daylight hours short. The smaller the bird the greater the amount of food in relation to body-weight that must be consumed. A Blue Tit *Parus caeruleus* weighing less than half an ounce may eat food in a day equivalent to 30 per cent of its bodyweight; the considerably larger Buzzard *Buteo buteo* as little as 4 per cent. The Woodpigeon *Columba palumbus* has been found when feeding on clover during midwinter to take no less than 35,000 leaves a day; those in late afternoon being stored in the bird's crop for digestion at night. That birds like owls hunt by night is well known; it is also a necessary habit for species which feed on the inter-tidal zone if they are to fully utilize the immense food source revealed by the receding tide.

All parts of the world, except for the highest mountains and the polar ice caps, have been exploited by birds for food. Thus, the bill, an extension of the jaws, has evolved into a great variety of types, each adapted for a particular mode of feeding. This can be clearly seen among waders on an estuary. Some species, such as the Curlew *Numenius arquata*, have long bills which can be used for probing at depth; others, such as the Dunlin *Calidris alpina*, have shorter bills which can still be used to probe, or equally to pick items off the surface. The recurved bill of the Avocet *Recurvirostra avosetta* is ideally suited for a sideways sweeping action through shallow water or slime. Oystercatchers *Haematopus ostralegus* are highly skilled at opening shellfish, taking less than a minute to cut the adductor muscle of a cockle and extract the soft body. The Turnstone *Arenaria interpres* uses its short bill to turn over small stones, seaweed or beach debris to reach the hidden invertebrate fauna.

Birds are quick to exploit new food sources. Witness the rapidity by which gulls are attracted to ploughing operations or the discarded lunch of a seaside holidaymaker. Blue Tits were first noted opening milk bottle tops to drink the cream near Southampton in 1921, a habit which has since spread and been learned by the Great Tit and Great Spotted Woodpecker.

Of all aspects of avian biology the migration of birds has captured popular imagination. Who can fail to be stirred by the annual journeys undertaken by many birds, including some of our smallest species? At the same time the impulses

Blue = Eurasation feeding area
Orange = Wintering area
for British Swallows

Distances covered by birds on migration are prodigious. British Swallows travel to and from Cape Province each autumn and spring.

which drive them to undertake these journeys, and the methods by which they reach their goals are still largely unknown.

Each March the Sand Martin *Riparia riparia* and Chiffchaff *Phylloscopus collybita* are among the first migrants to arrive in Great Britain. Numerous other species reach Britain during April and early May, a major one being the Swallow *Hirundo rustica* coming north from winter quarters in Cape Province.

Most of our other species will have wintered in the region immediately south of the Sahara. Moving north as spring advances they have come to breed throughout much of Europe and northern Asia. The long daylight hours and rich invertebrate supply enable them in some cases to rear several broods.

The arrival of spring migrants is a dramatic affair; they announce themselves by song as territories for the coming breeding season are established. By contrast, the autumn departure is more gradual and easily overlooked as the birds slip quietly away; however, the numbers leaving are staggering. Swelled by the year's young, it has been estimated that no less than 5,000 million birds from Europe and Asia (excluding water birds) move to winter in Africa south of the Sahara. Losses on migration and in winter quarters are enormous; only 2,500 million birds will return north to breed in the following spring.

The main barrier encountered by migrants heading north to Great Britain is the Sahara, involving a minimum direct crossing of about 900 miles (1,400 kilometres). Facing prevailing winds the birds may take between fifty and sixty hours to cross the inhospitable terrain with no hope of succour if grounded, so that flight has to be continuous until the Mediterranean coast is reached. The southward autumn journey, with the wind now of assistance, is usually accomplished in about thirty hours, but even so is a major feat for tiny birds like warblers.

Seabirds undertake equally spectacular journeys, the longest being that of the Arctic Tern *Sterna paradisea* which travels from its northern breeding grounds to spend the southern summer along the Antarctic ice-edge. The Manx Shearwater *Puffinus puffinus*, which breeds mainly on islands off western Britain, winters off Brazil, a journey of up to 6,000 miles (10,000 kilometres). Some individuals travel remarkably swiftly, the fastest being a chick ringed on Skokholm, Pembrokeshire, and recovered about thirteen days later off Brazil, an average speed of 460 miles (740 kilometres) per day. The Great Shearwater *P. gravis* and Sooty Shearwater *P. griseus*, both breeding in the South Atlantic, make equally lengthy northward movements and are regularly observed in summer off the coast of Great Britain.

# WHERE TO LOOK

## Mountains and moorland

The main upland regions in Great Britain are situated in the north and west, with the Scottish Highlands supporting the greatest variety of species, including some of the rarest. Among the rocky areas in the Cairngorms a few pairs of Snow Buntings *Plectrophenax nivalis* nest, climatic changes having reduced our population of this Arctic species.

Another bird of high ground in Scotland, though much more widespread, is the Ptarmigan, a game bird, mainly white in winter plumage. In summer the male has blackish brown upperparts, breast and flanks, a white belly, and in flight conspicuous white wings; females are more tawny. Great fluctuations occur in its numbers, peaks seeming to occur about every ten years. Despite increased human pressure at the breeding grounds the Ptarmigan seems to have suffered no ill-effects. Such disturbance on the mountain tops, however, adversely affects the Dotterel *Eudromias morinellus*. Nesting in areas with only sparse vegetation, mainly in the central

The mountains and moors of upland regions support a considerable variety of birds able to withstand the often extreme conditions.

Red Grouse

Snow Bunting

Dotterel

Highlands, this is one of our most approachable species. The male continues to incubate even when the observer is within a few feet of the nest.

Pride of place among mountain birds must go without question to the Golden Eagle *Aquila chrysaetos*, with a population of between 250 and 300 pairs, mainly in the Highlands and Western Isles. This is among the most sedentary of birds, remaining for the most part within its hunting territory, often close to the nest site or eyrie. During incubation the birds easily desert and the eyrie should not be approached at that period.

Although these species are all virtually restricted to Scotland, upland regions elsewhere are equally interesting. The Red Kite *Milvus milvus* occurs only in mid-Wales, where about twenty-five pairs breed although they continue to be harried by egg-collectors. Others, such as the Red Grouse *Lagopus lagopus*, Ring Ouzel *Turdus torquatus* and Wheatear *Oenanthe oenanthe* may be seen in most upland areas, even as far south as Exmoor and Dartmoor, where the former was introduced in the nineteenth century.

Golden Eagle

Ptarmigan

Agricultural land provides a variety of habitats, one of the most important being the hedgerow, disappearing all too quickly from our fields.

## Farmland

It was not until the late 1960s that it became generally recognized that farmland provides an important habitat, indeed a variety of habitats, for many forms of wildlife. Look at any farm and you can see fragments of habitats that were once much more widespread. Copses and shelter-belts provide woodland conditions, hedgerows and scrub, while no farm is without a pond, stream or marshy hollow. No less than 80 per cent of Great Britain is farmland of one type or another and how this is managed will affect a large proportion of our birds, mammals, plants and invertebrates. At the same time about 50,000 acres (20,000 hectares) are lost annually to urban and other development.

One farmland species, the Grey Partridge *Perdix perdix*, has undergone a spectacular decline in numbers throughout north-western Europe in recent years and this seems due to several factors. Alteration to the habitat, particularly when hedges, in which it chiefly nests, are removed is an important factor, as is the rapid ploughing in or burning of stubble which limits its autumn feeding areas. Invertebrates on which the chicks

Yellow Wagtail

Meadow Pipit

feed have declined as the agricultural weeds which supported them have been largely eradicated.

Hedgerows provide a nesting area for many birds particularly when interspersed with taller trees. No less than fifty-five out of the ninety species which regularly breed in lowland Britain use this habitat, though none is confined to it. Of these, seven, such as the Grey Partridge, nest on the ground; thirty, such as the Dunnock *Prunella modularis*, in bushes; and eighteen, such as the Mistle Thrush *Turdus viscivorus*, in trees. Some forage along the hedgerow and associated verges, others move into the fields. The most characteristic of the latter is the Rook which requires tall trees for nesting, but open fields on which to feed.

A few species breed on open ground, chief among these being the Skylark and Meadow Pipit *Anthus pratensis*, both occurring throughout Great Britain. Others may be more restricted, like the Yellow Wagtail *Motacilla flava*, a summer visitor, mainly to lowland England. Farm buildings attract several species, the most interesting being that most efficient of rat-catchers, the Barn Owl *Tyto alba*, which is unfortunately now rather scarce.

# Woodland

Since Neolithic times man has cleared some 90 per cent of British woodlands which now cover a mere 6 per cent of our land surface, so that we are one of the least wooded of European countries. Clearances were initially made to provide room for crops and animals, and then later for charcoal production and the supply of building materials, primarily for ship construction. Following the First World War the newly formed Forestry Commission embarked upon a replanting programme, mainly using conifers.

Woodland birds have thus faced centuries of continual change to their habitat, and in many cases of its complete destruction, but have nevertheless managed for the most part to adapt quite successfully. Some have moved to alternative areas – our hedgerows, parks and gardens – and none more so than the Blackbird, which is now more numerous in these habitats than in woodland.

Of our three resident woodpeckers only the Great Spotted has really penetrated our cities to occur amongst the inner suburbs and in parks. It comes regularly to feed on bird tables. The Green *Picus viridis* and Lesser Spotted Woodpeckers *Dendrocopos minor* are still mainly restricted to woodland, where, due to its retiring nature, the latter is often overlooked. The Nuthatch *Sitta europea* is another primarily woodland bird which occurs not infrequently in gardens and parks, although it is a scarcity near industrial centres, which has been attributed to soot limiting the insect fauna of tree trunks.

The Coal Tit *Parus ater* is one of the more numerous species, having increased its range as plantations have developed. Most birds prefer nest sites under rocks or among tree roots – coniferous plantations, having little or no ground cover, prove especially suitable. The Woodcock *Scolopax rustica* is a bird of open woodland with damp hollows, but it has increased its numbers in some areas due to the planting of conifers. During the breeding season males perform a display flight – 'roding' – when they follow a regular circuit, usually a little above the treetops, adopting a slow, owl-like wing-beat.

Woodland birds have adapted to continual restriction of their habitat, some species moving into urban zones as woods are cleared.

Green Woodpecker

Coal Tit

Great Spotted
Woodpecker

Nuthatch

Woodcock

Marshland holds an exciting number of birds, but is a fast disappearing habitat as swampy areas are reclaimed.

## Marshland

One of the most exciting habitats is without question marshland with its billowing reedbeds, shallow pools and wet meadows. Alas, for some of the birds which it supports, and the ornithologist who seeks them, only fragments remain, the rest having been drained. In Britain this has occurred not only in East Anglia, but also further west in the Somerset levels.

As such areas diminished some birds restricted to them declined in numbers, and in extreme cases ceased to breed for a while in Great Britain. Their disappearance was often hurried by the activities of nineteenth century egg collectors and sportsmen. The Bittern *Botaurus stellaris* disappeared in about 1868, but returned to breed in Norfolk in about 1910. Protection there and in Suffolk enabled it to slowly increase in numbers, while since the 1940s it has nested in several other counties north to Lancashire.

Both the Black-tailed Godwit *Limosa limosa* and Black Tern *Chlidonias niger* became extinct as breeding species before

Marsh Harrier

Sedge Warbler

Reed Bunting

the middle of the nineteenth century. The former re-established itself on the Ouse Washes, Cambridgeshire, in 1952 where protection and habitat management have enabled increasing numbers to nest with some forty-five pairs in 1974. Black Terns have nested sporadically in the same area since 1966.

The Marsh Harrier *Circus aeruginosus*, one of our rarest birds of prey, requires large undisturbed reedbeds in which to nest. During the present century breeding has been reported from at least eight counties, the peak being in the 1950s when there were about twenty pairs. Numbers have since declined to about three pairs, all in Suffolk. Destruction of reedbeds by coypu, human disturbance and the killing of migrating birds are considered responsible.

Smaller tracts of marshland successfully support widespread species like the Sedge Warbler *Acrocephalus schoenobaenus* and Reed Bunting *Emberiza schoeniculus*, the latter now increasingly found in drier areas. The elusive Water Rail *Rallus aquaticus* has a local breeding distribution, although it is probably often overlooked; more are seen in winter.

## Open fresh water

Great Britain seems particularly well endowed with areas of open fresh water. There are numerous lakes in the upland regions, though generally at too great an altitude and acidity to attract birds in any numbers. Natural open water in lowland Britain is less frequent, but man-made sources – reservoirs, flooded gravel pits and ornamental lakes – are found in most districts and are important for ducks and other waterfowl.

One of the most handsome species breeding at such sites is the Great Crested Grebe *Podiceps cristatus*, though little more than a century ago there were less than fifty pairs. Since then this species has increased in numbers so that by 1965 there were over 4,000 breeding adults. Most of the increase has occurred in areas where reservoirs and flooded gravel pits have provided new sites.

The Canada Goose *Branta canadensis* was introduced into Great Britain about 1660, and rapidly became popular as an ornamental waterfowl. In 1958 there were about 3,000 birds, but since then there has been a noticeable increase due to the

Flooded gravel pits are particularly attractive and abundant areas of open fresh water. Often breeding can be encouraged by the provision of floating rafts.

Great Crested Grebe

Shoveler

Tufted Duck

transference of birds to new areas by man. Most of our Canada Geese are sedentary, but for some quite unknown reason, those from the West Riding of Yorkshire make a moult migration each summer north to the Beauly Firth, Inverness-shire.

Safe nesting places for waterfowl have been provided at several sites by the provision of moored rafts. These usually measure about 70 square feet (6 square metres) and, covered with earth or shingle, they have proved most attractive. Perhaps the most exciting colonist has been the Common Tern *Sterna hirundo*, which, among other places has become established at a reservoir at the Shotton steelworks, Flintshire.

The greatest numbers of birds occur on inland waters during the winter months. The Coot *Fulica atra* is ubiquitous, the British stock being augmented in winter by continental immigrants. Diving duck, like the Tufted Duck *Aythya fuligula*, occur on most open waters, the largest concentration of this species being about 20,000 on Lough Neagh, Ulster. Among dabbling duck, the Shoveler *Anas clypeata* is also numerous on fresh water in winter, and as a breeding bird.

Canada Goose

Coot

## Rivers and streams

Waterways, whether natural or man made, like hedgerows, provide an important linear habitat for certain birds. Pollution is an obvious risk to any waterway, except possibly those in remoter upland regions. 'Algicides' and aquatic herbicides are now used more widely, and there is a possibility that 'piscicides' may be employed to remove coarse fish from trout streams. Destruction, or alteration of habitat when rivers are widened and vegetation cleared, can also affect several species.

The Dipper, a typical bird of fast-flowing streams and rivers, occurs only on more sluggish waters where weirs break the surface. Its habit of feeding while submerged, and mode of progress beneath the surface in at times turbulent conditions, has long been of interest. The wings are used underwater for swimming, although the bird may also walk along the bottom. Dippers feed in depths up to about 2 feet (60 centimetres), sometimes diving from flight or a prominent position, and at others simply wading in.

Two other species of upland streams are the Grey Wagtail *Motacilla cinerea* and Common Sandpiper *Tringa hypoleucos*. The former also occurs locally in lowland Britain where it suffered severely during the hard winter of 1962–63. The Common Sandpiper, its plaintive call and bobbing action attracting the observer's attention, is a summer visitor, and when on passage may halt briefly on estuaries or along rocky coasts.

The Kingfisher *Alcedo atthis* is normally found on slow waters where steep banks provide a suitable terrain for its tunnel nest site. Like the Grey Wagtail it also suffers during severe weather inland, and, each winter many move to the coast. The Sand Martin nests in similar positions, sometimes in colonies comprising several hundred birds. Sand Martins occasionally use other sites such as sand-dunes, but none is as strange as the colony beneath a platform at Ballinluig, Perthshire, close to the main railway line from Edinburgh to Inverness.

Where rivers regularly flood low-lying meadows, important wintering areas for wildfowl, in particular Bewick's Swan *Cygnus bewickii*, occur.

Rivers and streams support an interesting number of species, but are vulnerable to pollution.

Kingfisher

Sand Martin

Grey Wagtail

Dipper

Common Sandpiper

## Estuaries

Although comparatively few species of birds nest on or beside estuaries, this habitat provides an extremely rich winter feeding area for large numbers of waders and wildfowl. Some of the British estuaries – notably Morecambe Bay, the Solway, Wash, Ribble and Dee – are sites of outstanding international importance for waders. Unfortunately, like most other habitats, estuaries are liable to change brought about by man's activities; reclamation, human disturbance and barrage schemes can alter, and in extreme cases irrevocably destroy, the intertidal areas with their teeming invertebrate faunas on which the huge masses of birds feed.

It is probably the wader flocks which most people associate with estuaries, those in Great Britain holding a high proportion of the European population of several species. The Knot *Calidris canutus*, breeding no nearer than Spitsbergen, winters here in immense numbers, with no less than 388,000 in January 1972 (70 per cent of the European population). Our most numerous species is the Dunlin with 465,000 in the same

Estuaries offer wide areas of rich feeding for enormous winter flocks of waders and wildfowl.

Knot

Shelduck

Ringed Plover

month (45 per cent of the European population). Although not occurring in such large numbers, the Ringed Plover *Charadrius hiaticula* often joins with the Dunlin forming mixed flocks which frequently engage in spectacular aerial evolutions over the mud flats. The Sanderling *Calidris alba* is most often seen in May, when birds on passage from their wintering grounds beside the great lakes of East Africa pause briefly on our estuaries before continuing northwards.

Shelducks *Tadorna tadorna*, though feeding on estuaries, often travel several miles inland to breed and occasionally further, such as those that move up the Trent valley. In the late summer they undertake a moult migration to the great sandbanks of the Heligoland Bight, remaining there virtually undisturbed and for a time flightless, until the late autumn. All five species of terns regularly feed in our estuaries, and where suitable habitat exists will breed close by. Our largest species, the Sandwich Tern *Sterna sandvicensis* now thrives in several areas, notably Norfolk, due to the establishment of nature reserves, but has decreased due to human pressures in Scotland.

Sandwich Tern

Grey Plover

Sanderling

Kittiwake

Herring Gull

Rock Pipit

Cormorant

## Sea coasts

The coastline of Great Britain provides a home for almost uncountable numbers of seabirds, and as such it is the most important European country for this group of species. On the low-lying south coasts the Black-headed Gull *Larus ridibundus* and terns are the most numerous. The rocky shores of the north and west, where remote islands make even more suitable nesting sites, hold for some species the bulk of their North Atlantic population.

Two species of gull are among the most widespread of our seabirds. The Herring Gull *L. argentatus*, the familiar 'seagull', is at times anything but maritime and may forage far inland, particularly in winter, when it is attracted by such potential food sources as rubbish dumps and poultry farms. The greater amount of food now available has enabled it to increase, sometimes to the detriment of smaller seabirds. Herring Gulls are coming more to nest on buildings in coastal towns, although these still form only a small part of the total population. The Kittiwake *Rissa tridactyla*, which has also increased, is by contrast truly pelagic. Coming ashore only to breed, it forsakes its colonies during early September to roam the North Atlantic. Building a bulky nest of grass and mud, mainly on sheer cliffs, its clutch is normally two eggs – there would hardly be room for more chicks at such a precarious site.

Cormorants *Phalacrocorax carbo* breed on the coast, but regularly fly inland, sometimes for many miles, to fish on rivers, lakes and reservoirs, a habit which brings them into conflict with anglers. The smaller Shag *P.aristotelis* is much more maritime, occurring inland only when 'wrecked', and on such occasions often perches on prominent buildings.

A number of other birds occupies the coastal zone in addition to seabirds. The smallest, and often overlooked, is the Rock Pipit *Anthus spinoletta*, usually nesting in a hole or crevice close to the high-water mark. In northern areas the Eider *Somateria mollissima* can be encountered along the coast throughout the year. In some favoured bays large numbers of Common Scoter *Melanitta nigra* may gather.

The rocky coasts and remote islands of the north and west provide excellent nesting sites for many seabirds.

## Urban areas

Most birdwatchers quite obviously carry out their hobby in the countryside, but one should not neglect built-up areas. Among these, parks and gardens, playing fields, reservoirs and even sewage farms, provide a variety of habitats. An area where as many species, if not more, are seen during the course of a year, compared to any other, is that covered by the *London Bird Report*, covering a 20 mile (32 kilometre) radius from St Paul's Cathedral.

Most species move into urban areas in order to take advantage of the food and nesting sites man incidentally provides. The Black Redstart *Phoenicurus ochruros*, however, has been virtually restricted to the urban zone in Great Britain since it commenced nesting regularly about 1939. Confined mainly to the south-east, it found bombed sites in London and coastal towns like Dover much to its liking. Its numbers, never large, have declined as these have been cleared, and only a few pairs remain, their stronghold a large power station.

The Pied Wagtail *Motacilla alba* has been described as occupying the ecological niche of a walking House Martin. Certainly it seems as at home in a city street as in a farmyard puddle. At times large numbers have gathered to form roosts in cities, like that of over 3,000 birds in the trees of a Dublin street. Other favourite sites include the inside of commercial greenhouse roofs, while over 2,000 have been observed roosting on the moving distributor arms of a Reading sewage works.

Jackdaws *Corvus monedula*, formerly a crag- and tree-nesting species, find our tall buildings equally suitable, though rarely penetrate right into cities. The Collared Dove *Streptopelia decaocto*, first nesting in Great Britain as recently as 1955, now occurs in most city parks and suburban gardens. Sometimes large numbers become established and cause annoyance by their incessant loud calling and by damaging vegetables. Occasionally exotic species, escaped or liberated cagebirds, are encountered, but these rarely breed, unlike the Ring-necked Parakeet *Psittacula krameri*, which seems to have established itself recently in several south-east towns.

Do not overlook built-up areas in your search for birds. Urban areas offer a variety of habitats with associated species.

Jackdaw

Black Redstart

Collared Dove

Pied Wagtail

Ravens are among the earliest of nesters, beginning their breeding cycle as soon as January.

## WHEN TO LOOK

### Spring

Although winter visitors to Britain will not have departed and many resident species are still roaming the countryside in flocks, there are others which will be commencing their breeding cycle. One of the earliest is the Raven *Corvus corax*, now widely distributed in upland districts and along the cliff coasts of northern and western Britain. Greatly persecuted during the last century and driven from some areas, during more recent times it has increased, one sign of this being the number of tree nests now reported. The majority, however, uses ledges on cliffs, inland crags and quarries.

Some Ravens lay their eggs in early January and almost all will have done so by early March, the young fledging by late April or early May. Raven aerobatics over the breeding territory are without compare; their flight is powerful and if the air is still the loud swishing of their wings may be clearly heard. They play in the air, at times, I am sure, for the sheer exuberant pleasure of tumbling about the sky; at others, perhaps when driving off a passing Buzzard or Carrion Crow, their flight is equally dramatic. A long swoop at speed is made with wings half closed towards the intruder, followed by a rapid climb to gain altitude before the performance is repeated. On more relaxed occasions Ravens will dive in mock defiance at one another, their loud 'kronking' call notes seeming to give these spectacular displays a joyous air.

Two other early breeding birds are the Long-eared Owl *Asio otus* and Tawny Owl *Strix aluco*. The former is of local distribution only in Great Britain although it is probably often overlooked. Listen at night during the early spring in likely wooded areas for their low 'oo-oo-oo-oo' calls. The young, which leave the nest when about twenty-five days old, have a hunger cry best described as sounding like a rusty hinge. Tawny Owls are much more numerous, even nesting in city parks, although once again calling may be the only indication of their presence. Discovery of a nest, usually in a tree hole or occasionally in a ruined building or artificial site, is much more difficult.

With recent generally mild winters and early springs in Britain a number of species often commence breeding several weeks in advance of normal. Among garden birds the Song Thrush *Turdus philomelos*, Blackbird and Robin are always quick to take advantage of suitable conditions. Occasionally

An old barrel makes an attractive nest site for Tawny Owls which also breed early in the spring.

less likely species are recorded; a Hertfordshire Blue Tit laid its first egg on 10 February 1974, an exceptional date for a bird not normally beginning nesting until the end of March. Look out for such occurrences because they may be more frequent than realized.

As British resident birds really commence their breeding season so the first migrants arrive from their winter quarters. Two species of open country – the Ring Ouzel and Wheatear – are among the first to arrive from their African winter quarters and are normally reported early in March. The Sand Martin and Chiffchaff are a little later – the familiar call notes of the latter as it noisily announces its arrival is surely a harbinger of spring. By the end of March the almost identical Willow Warbler *Phylloscopus trochilus* and the Swallow will also have been seen. Although many such migrants remain to breed about our homes, many more push on north and for some the goal may be the Arctic Circle and beyond.

One of our ducks, the Garganey *Anas querquedula*, is an early migrant, unlike the others which are either resident or winter visitors to Britain. It winters mainly in West Africa, where along the Niger valley, its numbers may reach pest proportions among the rice fields. Less than 100 pairs nest in Great Britain, mainly in the south-east, though it regularly turns up elsewhere on passage.

Most of the other summer visitors to Britain appear during April, including the best known of them all, the Cuckoo *Cuculus canorus*. The call of this bird is difficult to mistake, but

The breeding season really gets underway with the arrival of the migrants. The Wheatear (*below left*) arrives in early March and the Spotted Flycatcher (*above*) in May.

beware of human imitators. The familiar House Martin also arrives in April together with other species like the Common Redstart *Phoenicurus phoenicurus*, Grasshopper Warbler *Locustella naevia*, Whitethroat *Sylvia communis* and Tree Pipit *Anthus trivialis*. Several others are not normally seen until May and among the last to arrive are the Turtle Dove *Streptopelia turtur*, Swift *Apus apus* and Spotted Flycatcher *Muscicapa striata*.

Since 1968 the numbers of several summer migrants have decreased, including the Sedge Warbler, Garden Warbler *Sylvia borin* and Yellow Wagtail. The Whitethroat has been the most affected and between the 1968 and 1969 breeding seasons numbers declined by no less than 77 per cent. This trend was also noted elsewhere in Europe. There has been no sign as yet of any recovery to the former population levels. Various suggestions have been made as to the reasons for this unprecedented calamity, including locust control programmes involving large scale spraying with insecticides, or adverse weather on migration. It is now generally agreed, however, that the drought on the southern fringe of the Sahara – the Sahel zone – where the Whitethroat winters, and where the human population has also suffered due to an absence of rain, is most likely to be responsible.

In this familiar April scene a watchful Mallard mother tends her lively brood.

## Summer

A great variety of animals builds nests, but birds are the most experienced and industrious. As the breeding season progresses so you can see, often at no great distance from your home, an infinite variety of nests, and the sites chosen to position them. Ground-nesting species include the Pheasant *Phasianus colchicus*, Skylark and, in more open terrain, the Curlew and Ringed Plover. Some merely line a scrape with vegetation and feathers, the Ringed Plover even uses small pebbles, shells and sometimes rabbit droppings for this purpose. The nests of duck such as the Mallard *Anas platyrhynchos* are among the most elaborate constructed by ground-nesting birds in Great Britain. They are usually situated in dense vegetation, sometimes at a considerable distance from water, and lined with copious amounts of dry vegetation and feathers. By contrast, a few species do not use any materials; both the Razorbill *Alca torda* and Guillemot *Uria aalge* simply lay their single eggs on the bare rock of cliff ledges.

The cup nests of species which use bushes and trees are variable. Some are delicately lined with moss and fine hairs and others may be decorated with lichens, such as that of the Chaffinch, perhaps as camouflage against predators. Larger species, for instance, the Carrion Crow and Rook, build bulkier nests

of strong twigs, but the interior cup is still lined with softer materials. Other birds choose holes, in particular the woodpeckers and tits, although they are generally not seen unless attracted to nestboxes.

Most intricate of all nests are those of the dome type, that of the Long-tailed Tit *Aegithalos caudatus* probably being the best known. It may be situated only 3 feet (1 metre) above the ground in bushes, or at over 60 feet (20 metres) in trees. The oval ball of moss, cobwebs, hair and lichen is lined with about 2,000 feathers collected from over a wide area. It seems quite remarkable that as many as twelve young may eventually emerge from the interior of this structure. Other dome nests, though of a less spectacular design, include those of the Wren and Willow Warbler. Even the House Sparrow may forsake a building to construct an untidy dome of straw in a hedgerow.

The Cuckoo occurs throughout most of Great Britain, the familiar call of the male and the bubbling of the female being heard until mid-June, after which the birds are silent. The birds frequent a wide range of habitats. On moorland the main host species is the Meadow Pipit, while in lowland areas birds such as the Robin, Reed Warbler *Acrocephalus scirpaceus* and Dunnock are parasitized. Each female Cuckoo normally lays up to ten eggs and is often vigorously attacked by the potential host as she searches for the nest.

The Greenfinch regularly rears two and sometimes three broods during the spring and summer.

The first young birds are usually seen during April, Mallard sometimes being encountered as they escort their broods of ducklings to the safety of water. Newly fledged young of certain species often gather into noisy feeding parties which forage along hedgerows or through woods. The tits generally predominate, although others join in; one observer encountered no less than fifty-five individuals of eight species – Great, Blue, Coal and Long-tailed Tits, Treecreeper *Certhia familiaris*, Goldcrest *Regulus regulus*, Siskin *Carduelis spinus* and Chaffinch.

Although we normally associate breeding birds with spring and early summer, many nevertheless extend their activities into July, August and even September. Among seabirds young Fulmars *Fulmarus glacialis* and Kittiwakes will be present and easily visible on their cliff ledges until early September. The late breeding of landbirds is often overlooked, but it nevertheless does take place, although may remain unobserved until newly fledged young appear. Many of those breeding in late summer are species which regularly have several broods, some being in the nest as late as September. The Greenfinch *Carduelis chloris* has a lengthy breeding season with second and even third broods not fledging until September. Many British migrants also have lengthy breeding seasons and manage to rear several broods. Both the Swallow and the House Martin regularly have three. The warblers which breed in Great Britain, particularly in southern counties, have two broods and it may be early September before the last leave the nest. Within a short period they will commence their hazardous southwards journey to Africa beyond the Sahara.

The first migrants start moving south about the beginning of July. Among the earliest are various waders. Whimbrels *Numenius phaeopus*, less than 200 pairs of which breed in northern Scotland, may be heard calling, sometimes far inland, as small flocks fly over. The Green Sandpiper *Tringa ochropus* tends to be more solitary; some may occur on passage even in late June, favouring small pools and the narrow creeks at the heads of estuaries. The rarer Wood Sandpiper *T. glareola* chooses similar sites. Some other waders will move from their breeding grounds to congregate in large flocks on estuaries or lowland meadows, the Lapwing often predominating.

Among the waders, however, the Green Sandpiper may be already winging its way southwards on autumn migration.

Cuckoos move south in early autumn to winter over a large area of central Africa (blue).

## Autumn

One of the first summer visitors to Britain to depart is actually also one of the last to arrive. The Swift is generally not seen in Britain until early May, yet after a mere twelve weeks some will be returning south at the end of July, and all but the occasional straggler will have left by late August. This is Britain's most aerial of birds, spending much of its time aloft. It is thought by some to fly at least 500 miles (800 kilometres) a day throughout the breeding season, after which it makes a journey to winter quarters which extend through much of

Africa south of the Sahara. One day the birds will be flying in screaming parties about our taller buildings, on the next all will be silent, the birds having departed.

Swallows and martins leave in a more leisurely fashion. Towards the end of their breeding season they gather in flocks, the Swallow in particular being most noticeable on telegraph wires and house roofs. Another favourite gathering area is among reedbeds where the birds also roost; in some districts many thousands of birds will be attracted. Up to 40,000 Sand Martins have been observed roosting in a Chichester, Sussex, reedbed, while much larger numbers have been recorded at some continental sites. Even while some birds are still feeding young, others will be passing through. Certainly during September the passage of Swallows and martins through Great Britain can be heavy, although stragglers will be seen until November.

While the departure of such species is a conspicuous affair, with daytime movements which birdwatchers can often observe along river valleys or beside the coast, other birds slip quietly away undetected. The Sedge Warbler and Chiff-chaff, for example, cease singing in late summer – the thick undergrowth and leaf canopy hides the birds and their time of leaving is usually unknown. Most of these species are nocturnal migrants and details of their movements become apparent only when the birds on passage pause at exposed sites, such as the bird observatories.

Early September is the time that Britain's most remarkable seabird the Manx Shearwater, leaves its colonies on the remote western islands and heads south, aided for part of the journey by the north-east trade winds, to winter quarters off eastern Brazil. The departure often coincides with rough weather as equinoctial gales surge in from the Atlantic. When this occurs many young shearwaters are blown inland, in extreme conditions right across Britain. Few that are 'wrecked' will survive, for grounded birds have great difficulty in taking off and are soon killed by cats or foxes, or die of starvation.

These same westerly winds sometimes bring strange migrants to the British Isles. Birds moving south along the east coast of North America may be blown off course – then, caught in fast-moving depressions, a few survive and reach

As autumn proceeds, numbers of Fieldfares and Redwings join us for the winter from the north.

Europe, much to the excitement and sometimes puzzlement of birdwatchers who encounter them. Waders are the most regular trans-Atlantic vagrants, the Pectoral Sandpiper *Tringa melanotus* arriving each autumn. Other visitors have included the Upland Sandpiper *Bartramia longicauda*, Lesser Yellowlegs *Tringa flavipes* and Buff-breasted Sandpiper *Tryngites subruficollis*. Even small passerines occasionally make the crossing and the Blackpoll Warbler *Dendroica striata*, Baltimore Oriole *Icterus galbula* and Song Sparrow *Melospiza melodia* are among those seen recently.

By early October winter migrants are arriving in Great Britain from their northern breeding grounds. Listen on still nights during October and November for the high-pitched 'seeih' flight calls of migrating Redwings *Turdus iliacus*. The Redwing is slightly smaller than the Song Thrush and easily identified by its darker plumage, pale eyestripe, reddish flanks and underwing. Redwings have nested regularly in Scotland since 1953, with about twenty pairs in 1971. The main winter influx, however, originates further north in the

Faeroes and Iceland, and to the east in Fenno-Scandinavia, the Baltic States and Russia. The Fieldfare *T. pilaris* is another winter visitor from much the same area and has nested here on several occasions recently. It often joins forces with the Redwing, the birds feeding extensively on berries from trees such as the hawthorn.

Chaffinches, Starlings, Skylarks and Meadow Pipits, though breeding widely in Britain, nevertheless also move in large numbers from the continent. They are mainly diurnal migrants, and flocks can often be seen generally moving west or south-west in the hours immediately after dawn. The Brambling *Fringilla montifringilla*, a finch breeding in Scandinavia, often mixes with Chaffinches, and may be located in overhead flocks by its loud 'tchuc' flight call. On the ground its white rump is conspicuous as the birds take off.

The Lapwing flocks, augmented by continental immigrants, are often joined by large numbers of Golden Plover *Pluvialis apricaria* with their melancholy 'tlui-i' calls, which, together with the plaintive cries of the Lapwing, can be heard on all British estuaries during the autumn. Flocks of Curlew and Oystercatcher also build up, the latter much to the annoyance of cockle fishermen on the Burry Inlet, Glamorgan and Carmarthen, who accuse it of damaging the shellfish beds.

Populations of our Lapwings and Golden Plovers are increased each autumn by fresh arrivals from the continent.

Lapwing

Golden Plover

The three divers occur off most coasts in winter and not infrequently on inland waters.

## Winter

The generally mild winters of recent years (that for 1973–74 was the warmest since 1934–35) are no doubt responsible for small numbers of summer migrants remaining in Britain instead of moving south. The numbers involved are only fractions of the total population, but they nevertheless seem to be increasing. Lesser Black-backed Gulls *Larus fuscus* normally winter in Iberia and north-west Africa, but some thousands can now be encountered both at coastal localities and inland where they regularly roost on reservoirs. The Greenshank *Tringa nebularia* has been remaining in Britain since the 1940s, and now about 500 occur in midwinter, half in Ireland and the rest on the southern and western estuaries. Among smaller species are two warblers, the Blackcap *Sylvia atricapilla* and Chiffchaff, the former visiting bird tables which enables it to survive any sudden cold snap.

The Black-throated *Gavia arctica* and Red-throated Divers *G. stellata* are among Britain's rarer breeding birds, with less than 150 pairs of the former, all in the west of Scotland. During winter birds from northern Europe move into Great Britain and occur in small numbers off most coasts – harbours, estuary mouths and sheltered bays being favoured. Each year a few are seen on reservoirs, including those around London. The Great Northern Diver *G. immer*, which has bred at least once in Scotland, is also a winter visitor, though rather infrequent in the south-east and rarely inland.

Great Britain provides important wintering areas for several species of wildfowl. Geese, though concentrating at traditional and usually undisturbed points, can sometimes be seen as they pass overhead en route for these areas. The Pink-footed Goose *Anser brachyrhynchus* is the most numerous, coming mainly from Iceland and Greenland and wintering to a large extent in central Scotland. In England the main concentrations are in Cambridgeshire, Cumbria and Lincolnshire. Two races of White-fronted Goose *A. albifrons* occur, the European being particularly numerous on the Severn estuary, while the Greenland winters mainly in the Hebrides and in Ireland. The Greylag Goose *A. anser* breeds in small numbers in north-west Scotland and at several localities in England where flocks have been introduced. Many more arrive in winter from Iceland to east and central Scotland, with a few crossing the English border.

Large flocks of 'grey' geese regularly winter at traditional undisturbed haunts.

Greylag Goose

Pink-footed Goose     White-fronted Goose

Nutcracker

Crossbill

female

male

Nutcrackers and Crossbills are sometimes driven from Europe to Britain by food shortages or adverse weather conditions.

The Wigeon *Anas penelope* is one of the most numerous winter ducks in Britain, with flocks of many thousands congregating on some estuaries. It often associates with the Dark-bellied Brent Goose *Branta bernicla*, the smallest goose to winter in Britain from the Arctic coasts of Russia and Siberia. In winter it frequents intertidal mud banks, searching for eel grass. This plant was almost wiped out in the early 1930s by a mysterious disease and, unable to find alternative food, the Brent Goose population seriously declined. Since the early 1950s numbers have been increasing with a world population of about 38,000 estimated in 1970–71. Brent Geese winter in comparatively few areas, the Essex coast being the main one.

From time to time 'invasions' into Great Britain of birds not normally seen, or seen only in small numbers, take place. One of the best known is that of the Common Crossbill *Loxia curvirostra* which breeds in the eastern Highlands, East Anglia and Hampshire. Invasions from Europe occur at varying intervals; there have been eighteen this century, the most recent being in 1973. These movements are probably a means of avoiding food shortage, sometimes as the result of a particularly productive breeding season. The first birds may arrive in midsummer, but others appear as late as December. Following such movements, Crossbills often establish themselves for several years in new areas, where they may be found breeding in midwinter, and in some cases with eggs by late January.

In the autumn of 1968 large numbers of Nutcrackers *Nucifraga caryocatactes* appeared throughout western Europe, with over 300 in Great Britain, more than five times the sum total of all our previous records. It seems that the birds had been driven from the Russian and Siberian breeding areas by a failure in the seed crop of the Arolla Pine, their main food source. The first birds were noted in early August, some eventually extending as far west as Glamorgan and the Isles of Scilly. A few survived until midwinter while several were reported in 1969. Many were emaciated on arrival and probably soon died, but others managed to survive, taking food as varied as mince from a butcher's shop to ants and wasps.

Winter sometimes sees the mass migration of common birds, perhaps even from the continent, during a sudden cold spell. The frosty or snowy conditions make feeding difficult, sometimes impossible, forcing birds to fly to the south or west to seek improved conditions. Among the species most regularly affected are the Lapwing, Redwing and Starling, and huge flocks of these can sometimes be seen passing over. If the western areas are also frozen, as occurred in the early 1960s, large numbers of birds unable to fly further may die.

# BIRDWATCHING EQUIPMENT

## Binoculars and telescopes

Although by providing food birds can be attracted to the house windows, and if time and patience and a little luck allow, some species can be stalked to close quarters, it is not long before the birdwatcher finds a real need for binoculars. You can dispense with many items of birdwatching equipment, but not binoculars. A good birdwatcher will always keep them close at hand to avoid missing interesting events. That bird of prey soaring overhead will pass out of sight before they can be brought from their case on top of the wardrobe, or the strange bird by the roadside will surely fly away while you rummage for them in the car boot.

Few people are fortunate enough to be able to disregard price. There are some good (though one must also add bad) inexpensive binoculars available at the present time, retailing from about ten pounds and at the other end of the scale, the ultimate in optical precision are binoculars costing up to two hundred pounds.

Binoculars have been described as a pair of low-powered telescopes mounted side by side, and having a central focusing

Always have a good look through a pair of binoculars before purchase. Avoid a pair giving bending at the edge of the field of view (*left*) or colour fringing (*right*).

screw. The squat shape is dictated by the need to reduce an otherwise impossible focal length by the use of glass prisms. Stamped on the body of the binoculars, usually close to the eyepieces will be the magnification and diameter of the object glass, written as $7 \times 50$ or $8 \times 32$ and so on. Do not rush into purchasing binoculars with a high magnification for it is much more important to choose those which have a good light gathering potential. This may be easily assessed by dividing the magnification into the object glass diameter; the factor obtained, known as the 'exit pupil diameter', should for preference be at least 5. For $7 \times 50$ binoculars this figure is 7, while for $8 \times 40$ it is equally suitable at 5. The amount of light gathered may not be too important on a bright day, but sooner or later you will be seeking birds in dense woodland or trying to identify a bird in rapidly fading conditions. This is when binoculars chosen with such eventualities in mind really come into their own. A further advantage is to purchase a model having 'bloomed' lenses which increase the light gathering powers, the 'bloom' normally appearing blue on the glass.

A good all-round binocular, suitable for use in a range of habitats from woodland to the sea coast, requires a magnification of about nine times. Weight and balance should be checked before purchase; it is surprising how heavy and difficult to hold steady binoculars can become when used for prolonged observations. The central focusing screw should be both easily accessible and adjustable. The field of view, usually given in the manufacturer's brochure or stamped next to the magnification also, needs to be considered. Some binoculars are termed 'wide angle', and are well worth the extra cost if you are often studying birds at close quarters.

Like any tool, to give proper service binoculars need looking after – a hard knock can upset the alignment of prisms, something adjustable only by an optican. Dirt or water, particularly sea water, on the lenses should be avoided, and cleaning must be done with care to avoid scratching the glass. Make sure all grit is removed using a soft brush before gently polishing with a cleaning tissue, chamois or well-washed handkerchief. Do not neglect the binocular strap – it is well worth purchasing a good one for cheap straps chafe through surprisingly quickly with sometimes disastrous results. Always insure your binoculars against theft or loss. The premiums are quite reasonable and can save much disappointment and spoilt birdwatching.

Most birdwatchers find that their binoculars serve them well on all occasions, but those who frequent estuaries and coasts sometimes require extra magnification. A telescope can then come in useful. With magnifications of up to sixty times, but with a small object glass, this instrument can be used only in good conditions. Its length and weight make handling difficult unless a tripod, or support from a fence, tree or seawall is used. The old type with three or four brass draw tubes is now largely superseded by shorter prismatic telescopes, though these are expensive instruments.

## Identification books

Anyone beginning birdwatching soon finds the need for a good identification book, and we now take their availability for granted. Yet as recently as 1931 E. M. Nicholson wrote: 'the satisfactory identification book for birdwatchers does not exist'. Indeed, two more decades were to pass before this omission was rectified. Until the early 1950s birdwatchers had to be content with books like T. A. Coward's *The Birds of the British Isles*, first published in 1920. Much smaller, and probably used by the vast majority of those adopting birdwatching as a hobby, certainly until very recently, was *The Observer's Book of Birds* by S. Vere Benson, first published in 1937. Unfortunately many of the birds portrayed in such books look somewhat stiff and posed, while not all are in colour.

In 1947 an identification revolution commenced with the publication in the United States of *A Field Guide to the Birds* written and illustrated by Roger Tory Peterson. The book was an instant success with a style which could be easily adopted in other countries. The same artist entered into collaboration with two British ornithologists – P. A. D. Hollom and Guy Mountfort – and in 1954 the first edition of the highly acclaimed *A Field Guide to the Birds of Britain and Europe* was published. Text was kept to a minimum, and appeared under three main headings: Identification; Voice; and Habitat. Maps of

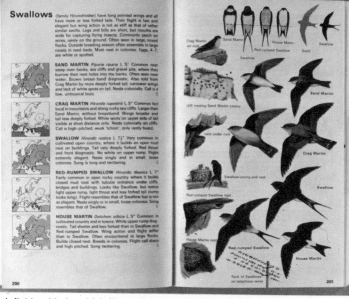

A field guide in which illustration, description and distribution map are arranged on one spread.

European distribution were included for all but those with restricted ranges.

It was with the illustrations, however, that the greatest advance had been made, though unfortunately even now not all were in colour. Instead of each species being shown separately, a whole series of related species was included on single plates. For instance, the ducks were divided up as surface feeders, diving ducks, sea ducks and mergansers, and shelducks, with additional plates showing flight features. Each species was shown as a simple sideways view, no attempt being made to 'pose' the birds, or to include background material. An important innovation, now known as the Peterson system, was the use of indicator lines drawing attention to salient features. For the male Mallard, lines showed the green head and white neck ring, and in the male Shoveler, the spoon-like bill and chestnut sides.

In 1970 *The Hamlyn Guide to the Birds of Britain and Europe* by Bertel Bruun, illustrated by Arthur Singer, was published. Covering a somewhat larger area than the earlier 'field guide' it has all but eight of the 519 species described illustrated in colour. Another distinct improvement in this work was the policy of having both the text and distribution maps on the page opposite the appropriate species illustration, which certainly makes the book a good deal easier to use. The plates are laid out in a more variable way than in the earlier 'field guide' and this, together with small supplementary illustrations, makes for a more pleasing appearance.

Yet another identification book was published in 1972: *The Birds of Britain and Europe with North Africa and the Middle East* by Herman Heinzel, Richard Fitter and John Parslow. Although an excellent book in many respects, covering such a wide geographical area means that many species hardly likely to occur in Great Britain, indeed in most of Europe, are included. For this reason I do not consider it suitable for use by the person just commencing birdwatching. However, the purchase of one of the other identification books mentioned is essential, and in view of the colour plates and ease of use I recommend Bertel Bruun's guide.

## Notebooks and record keeping

Together with binoculars and field guides the notebook is another important item of birdwatching equipment. It should be small enough to fit conveniently into a pocket; for many years I have found ones measuring $7 \times 4\frac{1}{2}$ inches ($18 \times 11 \cdot 5$ centimetres) most convenient for this purpose. A waterproof cover is well worth a few extra pence. It remains intact during the wettest conditions and the colour never runs, something which occurs with cheaper notebooks, often with disastrous results to clothing and other equipment. Always carry several pencils – in case one or more are broken.

Another useful aid in the field is the tally list or 'tick list' as it is often called. This printed list of bird names enables an easy record to be kept of all birds seen in an area, or on a particular day, by simply putting a cross or tick in the appropriate column. The British Trust for Ornithology (address on page 122) sells two such lists. The *Short British List* includes all the species one is likely to encounter during a normal day's birdwatching; it has two columns for records and is purchased in dozens. The *Complete British List* has six

The birds seen every day for a month in one locality can be recorded in a loose-leaf book (*top*). Printed tally list (*bottom*).

columns for records and is purchased in half-dozens. There is no end to the uses to which these lists may be put – birds in the garden, birds seen each year, birds on holiday.

A very interesting way of keeping records, especially if you cover the same ground regularly, for example, as you walk to school or work, is the daily tally list. A loose-leaf book is ideal. The bird names are written on the left-hand side of pages lying on the left. Narrower pages ruled to give thirty-one columns, one for each day of the month, are inserted as appropriate. Each species seen is recorded on the monthly sheet, so that over a period a most interesting and valuable record will result of birds in your neighbourhood.

The field notebook should not be looked upon as a repository for your records. At the first opportunity all information should be transferred to a more permanent source. Many birdwatchers simply write up their notes in diary form, a quarto or similar large format, stiff-covered notebook being particularly suitable. If you have a large quantity of information, however, a loose-leaf system, with a page for each species and possibly cross-referenced to a page for each locality, is a good idea. Certainly this is better than a card index.

# IDENTIFICATION

Most people can name a few particularly familiar or colourful species of birds; for instance, who does not know the Mute Swan *Cygnus olor*, Pheasant or Starling? A number of others may be placed into broad categories such as the 'sea gulls' though a little experience is required before the six species breeding in Great Britain can be identified. On taking up birdwatching it is not long before an unusual bird is encountered. It may be one well known to the observer but seen now for the first time in immature plumage or in moult, or it may be a completely new species. A written description must be made which can then be compared at leisure with those in various identification books. Thus, it becomes necessary to have a working knowledge of the topography or external features of a bird and this is not as difficult as it sounds, for it is simply knowing what the main features are called. All good identification books include drawings illustrating these points, and one is provided here.

You may refer to a particular part of the plumage as the 'back of the neck' but the 'nape' is a shorter and much more precise term used throughout the ornithological world. Likewise the 'rump' immediately denotes, without confusion, the extreme lower portion of the back and base of the tail. A companion hearing you on a field trip refer to the 'nape' knows exactly the area meant. A good birdwatcher learns all these terms, and to which parts they refer, at an early stage. Once this is done his or her verbal and written descriptions become precise and instantly comparable.

Many species can be distinguished only by the presence, absence or indeed combination of particular field marks. A birdwatcher should know of these and when particular attention needs to be paid to them. In the gulls the leg colour is an identification feature, while the bill colour of terns is of equal importance. The tail can also be important, particularly with regard to the amount of white that it carries. The Reed Bunting, for instance, has white feathers at the side of its tail, while the Whinchat *Saxicola rubetra* has prominent white patches at the base of the tail. Wing-bars and sometimes their

The external features of a bird (Chaffinch).

crown
forehead
ear coverts
lores
nape
mandibles
chin
back
throat
breast
flanks
rump
upper tail-coverts
belly
tibia
tarsus
under tail-coverts
toes
outer tail feathers

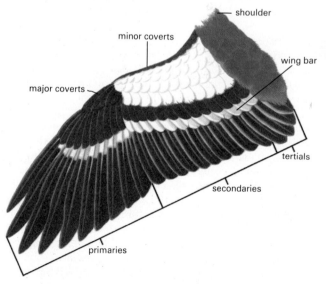

shoulder
minor coverts
wing bar
major coverts
tertials
secondaries
primaries

13 December 1974
Llys-y-fron Reservoir
Arrived 1030
Sunny, light wind from SW, water calm

2 Herons flying over from N
10 Cormorants, 1 on water, rest in trees
43 Coot in upper E arm

1 strange duck swimming with 4 Pochard and 17 Tufted Duck. Same size as others but tail lower on water.

Head shape different — rising steeply from base of bill to crown, then sloping gradually to back — almost triangular in shape.

Bill shorter than others.

Head chocolate brown, body grey, slightly mottled except for white collar on front of neck and 2 white patches on wing.

On flying off S, observed large white squares on upper surfaces of wings close to body.

Conclusion: female Goldeneye

An example of the notes taken during observation of an unknown duck. Later reference to a field guide enabled identification to be made.

combination with tail features are important for wader identification; in some species a good flight view may be necessary before the bird can be named.

Having learnt the names of the external parts of a bird and also something of the salient field marks, the observer is now ready to proceed with identification. It is not long before an unknown bird is encountered in the garden or during the weekend field trip. Do not take a few excited looks and then rush straight for the identification book. On turning to the plates showing species similar to your example, you may well discover that you had failed to notice a particular point which would have clinched identification. A further look through the binoculars reveals that the bird has gone and the puzzle remains unsolved. One's mind can also be surprisingly misled when looking at colour plates, so that a feature not really noticed may be imagined to have been present.

On encountering a new or doubtful bird, try first of all to

gather as much information as possible. Then, to prevent any possible confusion, make notes of your observations. Observation and note-taking *must* be made before any consultation with the identification book. If the bird remains in view it should be possible to obtain the maximum information, so that watching is interspersed with note-taking. Sketches, however rough, are often of help in clarification of plumage details. When accompanied by a friend, do not combine note-taking but act independently, because one may notice a feature overlooked or disregarded by the other. Two or more sets of notes are of much more value than a single combined record. Do not compare what has been written with colour plates and printed descriptions until you are completely satisfied that all possible observations have been made.

When taking notes there are two types of information to be sought but that gained from the immediate observations is most important. Probably the first point to be noticed is the bird's size, something which is surprisingly difficult to estimate with any accuracy, even at close range. It is much better to draw comparisons with other birds in the vicinity with which you are familiar; for instance, in a hedgerow the

When taking notes, draw comparisons with other birds in the same area. The shape and coloration of the female Goldeneye head, for example, is different from that of the Smew.

Smew female

Goldeneye female

Spotted Redshank

Redshank

Greenshank

Three similar-looking waders which can be separated in the field by careful observation of wing-bars, tail markings and by colour.

bird eventually identified as a Redwing was noted as being slightly smaller than a nearby Song Thrush. On the coast where confusion between the Cormorant and Shag can occur, a bird noted to be about the same size as the Great Black-backed Gull *Larus marinus* can only be the former.

Shape and posture are other important aspects which once again may be usefully compared with known species present in the vicinity. Does the bird in question stand upright, rather like the Spotted Flycatcher, or have a long, wagtail-like tail? Is it stocky or slender built, short-legged or long? Has it a thin or stout bill? These are just a few of the features which need to be looked for and noted. The bird's general colour should be recorded together with any particularly distinguishing marks, the field marks.

Waders on the estuaries can be confusing, though initial observations of size, shape and posture will immediately rule out some species. More detailed watching for wing-bars and tail markings may be necessary before a final identification is made. The following might be the typical sequence of observations during the identification of a Greenshank and a Spotted Redshank. A medium-sized wader of slender build, grey above and almost white beneath eventually takes off and flies down river one September morning, revealing a white rump extending in a 'V' wedge up the back. No white wing-bar is present and later observations include a loud 'tew-tew-tew-tew' call and olive-green legs.

A little further on several Redshank *Tringa totanus* are flushed, their white wing-bars and rumps clearly visible in flight. Among them a rather similar though darker bird is noted. The absence of wing-bars, and red legs trailing well behind, show this to be a Spotted Redshank *T. erythropus*.

The colour of the 'soft-parts' – the bill, legs, feet and eyes – should always be noted. Even the distribution of colour on these, as on the bills of terns, may assist in a correct identification. An Arctic Tern in summer has an all-red bill, with occasionally a little black at the tip, while the very similar Common Tern has an orange-red bill with a most definite black tip.

Notes on the behaviour and actions of an unknown bird are also of value when making an identification, so that

Willow Warbler

Chiffchaff

Willow Warblers and Chiffchaffs are so similar that only song, and, in the hand, close examination of the wing feathers enable identification.

besides making a record of size, shape, colour and field marks, watch what the bird is doing and how it performs various actions. If it is swimming, is it low in the water, its back almost awash, or does it ride buoyantly and erect? If it dives, how is this accomplished? For instance, both the Cormorant and Shag make a distinct up and forward spring before submerging, whereas the divers, with which these species might possibly be confused, simply lean slightly forward and disappear smoothly beneath the surface.

The way a bird takes off and how it flies can be just as important. Many surface-feeding ducks merely spring into the air, while some other species may have to patter their way over the water in order to gain enough flight speed. The Common Snipe when flushed has a most characteristic towering, zig-zag flight accompanied by loud, rasping calls. By contrast, the smaller Jack Snipe *Lymnocryptes minimus* has a slower flight, usually dropping back into cover within a short distance.

The song and call notes of many birds are so distinctive that they form a particularly valuable aid to identification. In some cases the bird betrays its presence by calling, and when good plumage views are unobtainable, its voice may be the only method of identification. This may occur when vegetation hides the songster, or if it is of particularly skulking habits, or when birds are flying overhead.

There are some closely related species so similar in appearance that they can be safely identified in the field only by voice characteristics. The Chiffchaff and Willow Warbler are both summer visitors to Britain, the former breeding north to the central lowlands of Scotland, the latter throughout the whole of Britain. In general appearance both species appear the same with olive-brown upperparts and buffish white underparts tinged with yellow. The voice of the Chiffchaff is instantly recognizable as a repeated 'chiff-chaff, chiff-chaff' sequence; the Willow Warbler by contrast has a soft musical song.

Although several of the tit family are among the most easily identified of small British birds, there are two so similar they provide the most expert with difficulties. The

The Coal Tit is distinguishable from the Marsh and Willow, but the latter two can give rise to confusion.

Coal Tit

Marsh Tit

Willow Tit

Coal Tit is easily recognized by its white nape and two narrow white wing-bars, but what about the Marsh *Parus palustris* and Willow Tits *P. montanus*? Looking so much the same, the latter was not found in Great Britain until 1897, the first being discovered as museum specimens labelled 'Marsh Tit'. Both breed throughout most of England and Wales and into southern Scotland, but not in Ireland, while their choice of habitat is a great deal wider than their names imply. Although the Willow Tit has a pale wing patch and a dull black cap, in contrast to the glossy cap of the Marsh Tit, these differences are usually hard to discern. Once again voice is a sure way of telling them apart, the Willow Tit having a loud 'tchay' and thin 'eez-eez-eez-eez-eez' notes. The main call of the Marsh Tit is a distinctive 'pitch-u-u', while it also has a scolding sequence.

It is usually possible to write down the main notes of many species in a manner in which they can be recognized by another person, but it is much more difficult to render songs in the same manner. Compare the versions for the same species in different books and you will see how interpretations differ. The best way of learning is to go into the field with someone who is already expert. When this is impossible the observer must be prepared to spend many patient hours, first managing to identify a bird, and then to learn its song and call note repertoire. A most valuable aid is the sound recording which can be played time and time again in your home. Most good shops have a selection of the many bird song records now on the market, while the local library may have some in its record lending department.

Developed in the United States, and incorporated in at least one of their identification books, is the visual reproduction of bird song – the audiospectrogram or sonogram. Made by a sound spectrograph, the diagrams may be reproduced in a book. For their interpretation a knowledge of music is helpful but by no means essential. First carefully study sonograms of birds with songs and call notes that are already familiar, before moving on to use the sonogram for unknown sounds. Practice like this will soon enable you to learn from a sonogram the pitch of an unfamiliar song in relation to a known one, together with the tempo and quality to be expected.

Grasshopper Warbler

Skylark

Sonograms illustrating differences in the one-note 'churring' of
the Grasshopper Warbler (*top*) and the more varied and melodious
Skylark song (*bottom*).

So much for the immediate observations. There are other
points which should always be noted and may assist in your
identification, or allow those whom you might consult to
clearly assess your description. Always record the habitat
and whether the bird preferred a particular sector of it. Date
and time of observation should also be noted together with
the weather conditions, particularly in relation to the visibility,
light and angle of the sun.

# FIELDCRAFT

Unlike many other animals, birds have a poorly developed sense of smell, but they have for the most part acute vision so that how a birdwatcher acts in the field, and what efforts are taken to become 'part of the scenery', will dictate how close he is going to get to the birds he wishes to observe. Binoculars enable you to watch birds from a distance, but there are always occasions when a closer view is required, which is something a well-planned approach will provide. The more inconspicuous you can become, the smaller the distance between you and the birds.

Look at the countryside; if it is summer then green of a variety of shades is the dominant colour. In winter when most leaves are shed and a good deal of ground vegetation is dead, brown takes over. When choosing the outer garments to be worn when birdwatching make sure they are a neutral colour, so that you merge with the surroundings. We can rarely afford a jacket for each habitat or season, or obtain those of reversible design – brown one side, green the other – which those pioneer bird photographers, the Kearton brothers, favoured. Choose something along the lines of dark khaki or lovat green, while the dappled camouflage jackets sold by some mail order houses are an excellent choice.

Bright colours may be suitable for mountaineering or water sports, but are easily visible at great distances, even in poor conditions, because that is their function. Birdwatchers, therefore, avoid reds, yellows and blues. If possible wear clothing in a disruptive patterning, a dark scarf, lighter anorak and darker trousers because such an arrangement helps break up the familiar human outline.

Of all parts of our form, the head, neck and shoulders are most typical, and are parts difficult to conceal satisfactorily in the field. We may crawl along a ditch or sprawl behind a seawall, but to make observations we have to reveal our upperparts. If we can disguise our characteristic outline then our opportunities may once again be improved. The simplest way is to put an anorak hood up, or to drape a coat over our head and shoulders, but attach neither tightly. Unfortunately, in windy conditions, both may be blown off or down in one's face. Better still is the camouflage hood invented by the

Reverend P. H. T. Hartley, which is simply an 'Arab head shawl' of green or brown to which are sewn small pieces of other suitably coloured material.

When moving about the countryside always keep below the skyline, and whenever possible keep the light behind you. This ensures the best viewing conditions with the maximum opportunity for concealment. Move slowly and always stand

Methods of disguising the 'give-away' head and shoulders outline.

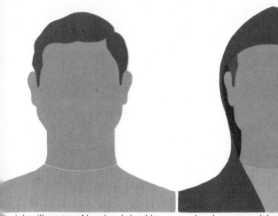

straight silhouette of head and shoulders

when loose anorak hood breaks up outline

a hat with brim helps

a camouflaged shawl or netting is most successful

75

in front of a tree or wall rather than look round it. A few minutes carefully studying your quarry, and the best route towards it, are usually well rewarded.

One way of providing concealment for watching birds is by using a hide. These are usually portable, though on occasions a more permanent structure can be situated at a particularly favourable point. Perhaps there is a pond in the secluded corner of a field where a sympathetic farmer may allow you to construct a hide. Permanent hides, however, are usually to be found only at ornithological reserves; the tree hide at Minsmere, Suffolk, and the tower hides of the Wildfowl Trust in Gloucestershire and elsewhere, are among the best known.

A car makes an ideal mobile hide within limitations. Pulling into the side of a quiet country lane can prove very rewarding, especially near to a gate or low section of hedge, when the birds will usually continue to go about their affairs quite unconcerned. I have found a car particularly useful as an observation point on roadside estuaries. If you leave the vehicle, however, the birds immediately become nervous and move further away.

If you continually use the same spot from which to watch, perhaps a favourite position on a seawall, or behind some lakeside bushes, then you can often improve the situation by constructing a 'sconce'. Nothing elaborate is required – a low pile of stones with a space near the base for viewing is ideal on a seawall. The addition of a few handfuls of reeds to bushes in winter can often make up for a lack of leaves, and aid the observer in remaining undetected.

A portable hide is reasonably easy and cheap to construct, while there are commercial designs currently advertised in the bird magazines. If you decide to make your own the points to remember are that it should be light, easily erected and dismantled, and lightproof. The best material to use is tent canvas of a suitably neutral shade, but to minimize cost still further strong hessian will suffice. In this event it must be lined to prevent the observer being visible, while it is also a good idea to waterproof the roof by incorporating a sheet of

Hides enable observation of birds at close quarters. An easy-to-make portable design is shown here.

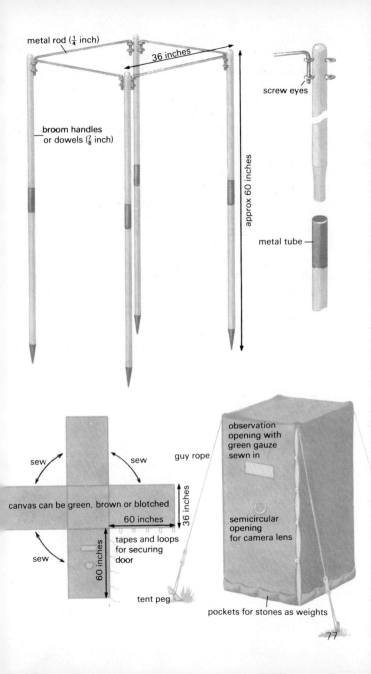

metal rod (¼ inch)

36 inches

screw eyes

broom handles or dowels (⅞ inch)

approx 60 inches

metal tube

sew

sew

sew

canvas can be green, brown or blotched

60 inches

36 inches

60 inches

tapes and loops for securing door

tent peg

guy rope

observation opening with green gauze sewn in

semicircular opening for camera lens

pockets for stones as weights

plastic. Guy ropes are necessary at each corner and the sides should not billow in the wind. Camouflage in the form of vegetation can easily be added and helps break up the regular outline.

Hides may be used in a great variety of situations, but are probably at their greatest value when sited for observation and photography at the nest (see also pages 108–9). Mention should be made at this point that some seventy of the species breeding in Great Britain are listed in the First Schedule of the Protection of Birds Act, 1954. Anyone wilfully disturbing these birds at the nest is liable to a fine of up to £25. Although most are rare, several not even regularly nesting, there are others which even a beginner may discover, in which case the locality *must* be avoided (see pages 112–13 for further details).

Discovering nests, even of the common species in our gardens and nearby hedgerows, can be a most rewarding and exciting aspect of birdwatching. Indeed, some birdwatchers specialize in this, becoming highly proficient, and discover species and information concerning them which most of us pass by. Although the nests of a few species may be easily found, others require a high degree of expertise and patience. There is now an excellent book available on this subject – *A Field Guide to Birds' Nests* by Bruce Campbell and James Ferguson-Lees –

The contents of an otherwise inaccessible nest can be viewed using a home made 'mirror stick'.

which is a mine of information, and useful for all birdwatchers whether or not they search for nests.

Most birdwatchers wear suitable clothes when pursuing their hobby, but those who have nests as their quarry should doubly ensure that they are appropriately dressed in their oldest but stoutest garments. This aspect of birdwatching continually leads the observer into the thickest nettle beds, bramble brakes, thorn coverts and marshes. A good stick is a necessity and is put to a variety of uses. Tapping posts, tree trunks and even the ground gently flushes sitting birds, while the stick also proves excellent for parting vegetation, or for replacing it as the nest site is left. An adjustable attachment by which a mirror, one of about three inches (7·5 centimetres) diameter is ideal, may be fixed to the end of the stick, is of value. This can then be used to view the contents of nests otherwise not accessible, or where a close approach may damage the site.

Many nests cannot be viewed from the ground, being constructed in tall bushes, in trees or on cliffs and crags. In attempting to reach such nests *extreme caution must be exercised at all times*, even on the shortest climb; discipline will then come naturally as you proceed to more hazardous situations. A light extending ladder is useful, but far too cumbersome for general use. The observer will therefore need to rely on climbing skill, requiring a fair degree of strength in arms and legs, and of course a head for heights. In some situations the use of a rope and assistance will be required, and it is probably best to have a friend standing by when climbing. Always study the proposed ascent carefully before proceeding for this will save much wasted effort. As it is easier to ascend than descend, make sure hand and foot holds are easily found and not too far apart. A golden rule of climbing is to ensure that the body is supported by three limbs before moving the fourth.

Aquatic habitats can be equally tricky; once again a stick is valuable as a probe to test the immediate area you wish to cross. Beware of sudden changes in water depth, and for this reason anyone entering water is well advised to be able to swim.

A few birds – some seabirds, the Rook and House Martin – nest in such conspicuous sites that nests can be located easily.

Many others provide clues when they are nesting and knowing these, and how to apply them, can mean that a population or area may be assessed for its breeding birds without actually having to locate the nests. This is also the first step in nest finding – that of locating breeding birds in their habitat.

Most birds give loud alarm calls when the area of the nest is approached, either by human intruders or the potential predator. In some instances the birds will perform distraction displays to lure the threat away from the eggs or young. Such displays usually take the form of injury feigning, where one or both adults will pretend to be injured or ill. Birds which have developed this habit are mostly species nesting on, or close to, the ground. The Oystercatcher can become almost hysterical in its calling if danger threatens its young, and will tumble about on the ground dragging a wing in a most convincing manner. Several other waders, which also breed in Great Britain, feign injury including the Golden Plover, Dotterel and Common Sandpiper. Both the Black-throated and Red-throated Divers will fly off normally when flushed from their eggs, but may drop suddenly after a few yards as though shot. Even small birds like the Willow Warbler will try to deceive the observer.

Behaviour like this is a sure sign that the birds are breeding close by, and can be followed up if required by a search for

A male Stonechat seen regularly carrying food in a particular direction will probably lead you to its nest and young.

the nest. When gathering nesting material birds can often be watched from different points as they return to the nest. When both birds of the pair brood the eggs, observations during the incubation period may reveal when the changeover at the nest occurs. Be prepared for long hours of watching, however, as this takes place infrequently. When only the female incubates she may leave the nest to meet the male to feed before being escorted back. Some males actually feed the female as she incubates.

Once the eggs have hatched, the hectic food collection means that careful watching of adults back to the nest may reveal its position. Concentrate your attention on where the bird leaves cover after taking food in, rather than where it entered. Birds carrying faecal sacs – the droppings of many young birds are enclosed in white gelatinous envelopes for easy removal – may also help in revealing a nest site.

Well-grown young can often be heard calling from the nest – Starlings are particularly noisy in this respect. Parent birds, which during the earlier stages may have been silent, can become noisy as their young approach fledging, their agitation signified often with loud scolding notes.

Nests may also be found by what is termed 'hot searching', the aim being to flush sitting birds, and this is the only method for some species nesting in low situations or of a particularly secretive nature. Using a stick, vegetation is gently tapped, the observer then waiting for the bird to appear. In open country a rope may be dragged by two observers with a third following up behind in order to see where the birds break cover. 'Cold searching' is simply searching in likely areas for nests, which in hedges are best seen when looking through against the light.

Observers must approach nest finding with a sense of responsibility, with the birds' interests paramount, however desperate they may be to gain further knowledge. Visits to any nest must be kept to a minimum; a little noise made on the approach gives the sitting bird warning and a chance to slip away unobtrusively. Natural predators are quite able to find nests that do not have tracks leading to them, but such tell-tale marks will guide children to nests so extra care must be taken to avoid leaving these.

# FURTHER STEPS

## Berries for birds

The larger your garden or piece of ground, the more scope you will have for 'bird gardening'. Wild shrubs like Blackberry, Elder and Hawthorn provide a rich berry crop and should be encouraged and indeed introduced whenever possible. For most of us, however, the garden is too small to allow such plants to run riot, but it is usually possible, even in restricted areas, to plant ornamental berry-bearing shrubs which birds find attractive. Not all berries are edible, but care taken when ordering should ensure, once the plants are established, a regular and increasing food source which certainly attracts birds into the garden.

In a survey organized by the Royal Society for the Protection of Birds observations were submitted covering the feeding activities of birds on no less than 135 species and subspecies of plant. Natives, as was to be expected, figured most highly on this list. No less than thirty-two species of birds were noted feeding on Elderberries, twenty-three on Hawthorn and seventeen on both Blackberry and Yew. Besides the latter,

*Cotoneaster* berries are a popular food source among birds in autumn and particularly with Waxwings.

birds were also noted feeding without ill-effect on several other species with berries that are poisonous to most animals.

Among ornamental shrubs the cotoneasters are great favourites with a wide variety of birds, ranging from the House Sparrow to the Mistle Thrush, and may even attract rarer visitors such as the Waxwing *Bombycilla garrulus*. Native to the Himalayas, cotoneasters were introduced into this country in the nineteenth century and many varieties are now available which thrive in virtually any soil and position. Among the best for birds are *Cotoneaster horizontalis, C. simonsii,* and *C.* x. *watereri.* Two dwarf species normally not exceeding twelve inches (30 centimetres) in height, and so ideal for rockeries, are *C. dammeri* and *C. prostrata.* The berries of several others are not quite so attractive to birds and may not be taken until other sources have been utilized, but should be planted with midwinter feeding in mind. These include *C. frigida* and *C. rothschilda.*

The familiar Mountain Ash or Rowan of western Britain is regularly planted in gardens, parks and avenues in several varieties, the berries of most of which are eagerly sought by members of the thrush family as soon as they ripen. A good purchase for small gardens is *Sorbus vilmorinii*, generally not growing to a height of more than 12 feet (3·6 metres). To be avoided, from a bird's point of view, are several whose berries are never eaten, including *S. hostii, S. hupehensis* and *S. mougeatii.*

Berberis with both magnificent foliage and a good berry crop, are easily established shrubs requiring a minimum of attention. *B. aquifolium* and *B. darwinii* are perhaps the best varieties. The firethorns *Pyracantha* provide a food source which may last until January. Flowering crab apples *Malus*, although not suitable in small gardens, do provide a first-class supply of food, normally not utilized until midwinter, for several species of birds. Similarly, Holly *Ilex aquifolium* berries tend to be left until other, softer fruits have been consumed. Honeysuckle *Lonicera* berries are much sought after by birds, including summer visitors like the Blackcap. When trained up a wall or over a trellis Honeysuckle also provides a nesting place for Spotted Flycatchers; indeed many of the other shrubs planted for their fruit can serve a similar dual purpose.

## Feeding birds

Berry-bearing shrubs and trees can provide food for a limited period only and may not be suitable for some birds. Another way by which birds may be attracted to the garden, or indeed to any spot, is by the provision of a feeding station. This is usually a bird-table, hanging feeder, window ledge tray, or simply an open area where food is regularly scattered on the ground. At one time little more than table crumbs were put out for birds; nowadays feeding birds is highly developed with commercial feeders and food in bulk advertised. Many people feed birds, deriving great pleasure by doing so and at the same time assisting the bird population at times when more natural foods are scarce, or possibly unobtainable, in hard weather.

A bird-table is easy to make, the only tools required being a hammer, saw and screwdriver. A very basic design is shown opposite. If you have the skill, embellishments such as a roof may be added, although this is not essential. The feeding tray should be at least 4 feet (1·2 metres) from the ground, into which the support post, suitably treated with a wood preservative, is embedded for at least 18 inches (45 centimetres). Despite the retaining ledges, untidy feeders such as the Starling soon scatter food on to the ground where birds are vulnerable to the ubiquitous cat; danger from this lethal source may be minimized by situating the bird-table at least 3 yards (3 metres) from the nearest cover.

The traditional bird-table is available commercially together with smaller hanging models. Various other feeding devices are currently on the market, the favourite being the tit feeders, the simplest no more than a wire or plastic mesh basket filled with nuts. Others may be more elaborate, but all give scope for these birds to display the agile antics which make them so entertaining when feeding. Although of immense value in winter, feeding is not recommended to any large degree during the summer when natural foods normally abound and provide the correct diet for nestlings.

Table scraps form the basis of much that is put on the bird-table, wholemeal being much more preferred than white bread. Cheese and fatty items, grain and bird seed, nuts and chopped apples are all greatly appreciated. Feeding birds in the

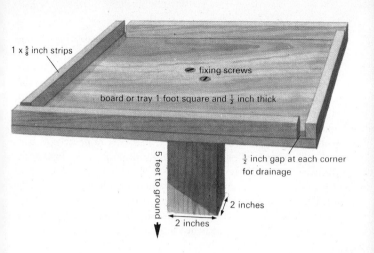

1 x ⅝ inch strips

fixing screws

board or tray 1 foot square and ½ inch thick

5 feet to ground

½ inch gap at each corner for drainage

2 inches

2 inches

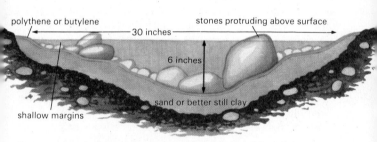

polythene or butylene

stones protruding above surface

30 inches

6 inches

sand or better still clay

shallow margins

Birds can be attracted into your garden by the provision of a feeding table or place to drink and bathe. Both are easy to construct.

garden may bring you into contact with species normally not encountered there, such as the Great Spotted Woodpecker, Reed Bunting and Siskin. The latter seems to have recently acquired a liking for peanuts from red plastic containers.

Birds need water for bathing and drinking and a garden pond with shallow margins is ideal. Alternatively, a small hollow lined with thick plastic, as shown above, or a shallow tray, will suffice. Ensure any ice is removed in winter from the water which is still required at this time.

# Nestboxes

There can be few greater enjoyments in birdwatching than that of a pair of birds successfully nesting in a box, or at an artificial site which you have provided. Among the earliest to be used were improvements in the Middle Ages to cave ledges where Rock Doves *Columba livia* nested, the squabs being collected for food. A similar use was made of young Sparrows and Starlings reared in wooden and clay flasks, in both Holland and Silesia. In Great Britain a pioneer of nestboxes and specially prepared sites as a means of attracting birds for pleasure was Charles Waterton (1782–1865) of Wakefield, Yorkshire. Besides nestboxes he had a wall specially built with holes for Sand Martins and a 'ruin' constructed for Barn Owls. Nestboxes for the Great and Blue Tits are most popular.

A nestbox of this type is not too difficult to make, requiring few tools and a minimum of carpentry skill. Alternatively, several firms and the Royal Society for the Protection of Birds offer various types for sale. Anyone with room for more than one or two boxes may find costs too great other than by do-it-yourself. There are a number of variations in the basic design and these, together with the many other types, are clearly illustrated and their construction detailed in an admirable booklet *Nestboxes* published by the British Trust for Ornithology. This is recommended for anyone building nestboxes.

The timber used in any nestbox should be at least $\frac{3}{4}$ inch (2 centimetres) thick, but need not be planed. Having cut the timber to size, the sections are nailed together using $1\frac{1}{2}$ inch (3·8 centimetre) nails. Always ensure the base is fitted between the sides as this prevents rain seeping in and causing the nest to become damp. A sealing compound, available at any ironmonger or do-it-yourself shop, should be applied to each edge before nailing; this will ensure that any irregularities in the timber are made draught- and damp-proof. The removable roof must overlap the sides to exclude rain, while some types have the whole front hinged as a door. In this case a retaining bar needs to be inserted low in the entrance to ensure that on opening the door the nest is not dislodged.

The size of the entrance hole is important, and you can normally arrange for this to be cut by a carpenter. It should be situated about $1\frac{1}{2}$ inches (3·8 centimetres) below the roof

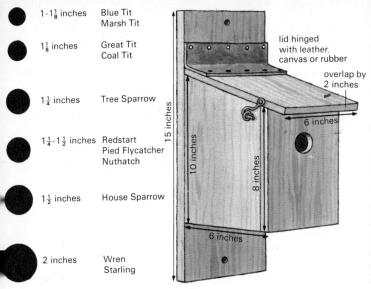

| | | |
|---|---|---|
| 1-1⅛ inches | Blue Tit Marsh Tit | |
| 1⅛ inches | Great Tit Coal Tit | |
| 1¼ inches | Tree Sparrow | |
| 1¼-1½ inches | Redstart Pied Flycatcher Nuthatch | |
| 1½ inches | House Sparrow | |
| 2 inches | Wren Starling | |

This is a typical nestbox suitable for tits, with recommended diameters for other species.

and, if Great or Blue Tits are the required occupants, it needs to be about 1⅛ inches (2·8 centimetres) in diameter. Anything larger than this may be entered by unwelcome guests such as House Sparrows, although for nesting this species requires an entrance of about 1½ inches (3·8 centimetres) diameter. Boxes may be attacked by squirrels and woodpeckers which often try to enlarge the nesting hole; this can usually be prevented by lining the interior adjacent to the hole with a strip of non-rust metal.

Apply a coat of wood preservative to the exterior, but never the interior, of the nestbox prior to erection, which should if possible take place during the autumn. This gives it time to weather and to become 'part of the scenery'; some boxes indeed may be used for winter roosting. Even those put up in early spring may be speedily occupied if natural holes are scarce, but you may otherwise have to wait until the following year. Nestboxes should be placed where they are at least partially shaded from the sun, and should tilt slightly so that the entrance is shielded somewhat from driving rain.

Nestboxes may be put up close to the house, even on the wall itself, but do not become too enthusiastic if you live in an urban or suburban area; here one, and at the most two, boxes in the garden will be sufficient. Observations have shown that Blue Tits in this habitat rear smaller broods than those in woodland where natural foods are more plentiful. Visit the box infrequently, taking special care near to fledging time in case the young leave prematurely.

If you have more scope than a garden in which to work – a section of woodland or open country with hedges, for example – there are many opportunities for nestbox construction with a view to encouraging a variety of species. Quite a number of birds, not normally associated with man-made sites, can be persuaded to nest if suitable designs are made available. These include duck, though you can hardly hope for Goldeneye *Bucephala clangula*; among the first to have nested in Great Britain was a pair at a nestbox in Inverness-shire in 1971.

Birds of prey and owls are possibly the most exciting species attracted to nestboxes, that for the Tawny Owl being easiest to make. This is just a wooden chimney about 30 inches (78 centimetres) in length by 8 inches (20 centimetres) square. At one end a piece of metal with a few perforations for drainage is attached. The box is attached at an angle of some 30 degrees from the vertical beneath a sloping limb, and so simulates a hollow broken branch. Tawny Owls will also nest in barrels (see page 43) or even boxes wedged into trees. Kestrels *Falco tinnunculus* seem to like large, open-fronted boxes in trees or even mounted on poles in open country, while in 1973 a pair nested in a box on the thirty-third floor of a London office block.

The Willow Tit each year chisels out its own nesting hole in the soft interior of decaying branches and trunks, but can be attracted to the normal tit box when filled with expanded polystyrene, now widely used as a packing and insulating material. This seems to be readily accepted as a substitute and the birds easily hack out a nesting cavity. Woodpeckers are not so easy to accommodate, though both the Great and Lesser Spotted have occasionally been attracted to large boxes packed with polystyrene.

Some examples of other types of easily constructed nestboxes.

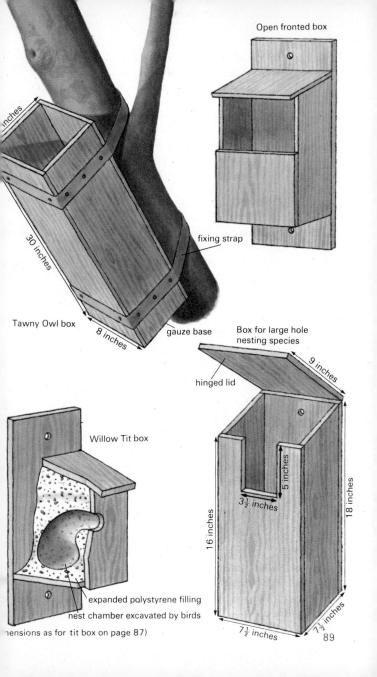

Open fronted box

Tawny Owl box

fixing strap

gauge base

30 inches

8 inches

Box for large hole
nesting species

hinged lid

9 inches

Willow Tit box

5 inches

3½ inches

16 inches

18 inches

expanded polystyrene filling

nest chamber excavated by birds

(dimensions as for tit box on page 87)

7½ inches

7½ inches

89

# Nest records

Every time that we examine a nestbox or discover a nest, we are certain to make a note of its contents, counting the eggs or young which it contains. Sometimes the details are merely commented on and with the passage of time forgotten. Some birdwatchers, however, will make a written record in their diaries or filing systems and this is most valuable, enabling interesting and important information to be accumulated.

Nearly forty years ago a keeper at Whipsnade Zoo, E. S. Billett, kept detailed records of all the nests in the bird sanctuary. From this pioneer work the late Dr (subsequently Sir) Julian Huxley and James Fisher devised in 1939 the 'Hatching and Fledging Scheme' for the British Trust for Ornithology. Now called the 'Nest Records Scheme', it receives over 20,000 completed cards annually from birdwatchers in Great Britain, while over thirty other countries have followed this example and now have their own schemes.

In its early years the main information derived from the completed cards related to length of incubation and fledging periods, which for many species at that time were imperfectly known. As more data have been accumulated it is possible for detailed analyses to be made which tell us a good deal concerning clutch size, fledging success, predation and population levels. The scheme helped reveal the tremendous decline in our Whitethroat numbers between 1968, when 326 cards were submitted, and 1969, when there were only 45.

At the end of 1972 the grand total of nest record cards received for the Blackbird numbered no less than 64,022, with 40,200 for the Song Thrush. The Dunnock, Swallow, Blue Tit and Linnet *Acanthis cannabina* all had totals exceeding 10,000. At the other end of the scale only a handful of cards has been received for rare species, or those like the Water Rail, Nightjar *Caprimulgus europaeus* and Rock Pipit, whose nests are difficult to locate.

Most of the cards submitted to the scheme are completed by members of the British Trust for Ornithology, but any birdwatcher able to identify and make accurate notes concerning nests may contribute. There is a most excellent field guide concerning the scheme, available from the Trust from whom nest record cards may be requested. These should be completed

A completed nest record card.

| OBSERVER: Robert Saunders | SPECIES: Blue Tit | YEAR: 19 74 | B.T.O.Ref. |

| DATE Day / Month | G.M.T. | EGGS | YNG. | NO. of EGGS or YOUNG at each visit. Record here stage of building; if bird sitting; if eggs warm; age of young; ring nos. etc. |
|---|---|---|---|---|
| 9 APRIL | 1800 | | | building 1/4 |
| 13 " | 1555 | | | building 1/2 |
| 19 " | 1240 | | | building complete |
| 24 " | 2110 | 4 | | bird on |
| 28 " | 1935 | 7 | | eggs cold and partly covered |
| 1 MAY | 0910 | 7 | | bird on |
| 6 " | 1750 | 7 | | " " |
| 21 " | 1600 | | 5 | " " |
| 28 " | 1700 | | 4 | |
| 2 JUNE | 0900 | | 4 | young leaving |
| 3 " | 0900 | | | nest box empty |

COUNTY: Pembroke

LOCALITY (place-name): Sunnyhill Rosemarket    Grid Ref: SM948087

ALTITUDE above sea level 100 ft.

HABITAT: Delete those inapplicable:- RURAL/~~URBAN~~

Hedgerow close to disused railway line and scrub covered bank

NEST SITE: In nest box on ash tree

Further visits, notes on outcome, etc. – ON BACK

Height above ground or cliff-base 5 ft

for any nest of which the contents have been counted at least
once, though to gain the maximum information several well-
planned visits are necessary. The observer should not complete
cards for interesting nests only, but for *all* nests discovered,
to avoid giving the data a bias.

If possible, nests should be located when the birds are
building, and then several visits, preferably in the afternoon
or evening, are required to establish when the first egg is laid.
The next visit is during the incubation period so that the full
clutch may be ascertained. Some clutches may already be
completed when discovered, and then visits every three days
will ensure that the hatching date is learnt. A further visit
about three days after this will reveal the number of young
which hatched, and another about the three-quarters' stage
will provide the family size. No approach should be made
after this in case the young are frightened into leaving
prematurely, though observation is sometimes possible from
a distance. A further check is made once the young are flying
to ensure none died, and observations should be maintained at
intervals until July or even August to see whether more broods
are reared.

## Surveys and censuses

For a few birds it is possible to locate all nests in a given area without too much difficulty; here the accent being on a population survey, rather than a detailed examination of nest contents. The easiest of all such species to which this may be applied in Britain is the Rook. As part of a wartime investigation into the economic importance of this bird, a survey of rookeries was made in 1944. Since then repeat counts have been made in several counties and a full survey was undertaken in 1975.

Nests are in most cases conspicuous and easily counted before being hidden by leaves from mid-April onwards; the colonies are mostly situated in shelterbelts, hedgerow timber and small woods. Some are extremely large, like that at Hatton Castle, Aberdeenshire, with over 6,700 nests in 1957; most, however, number less than 100 pairs, while single nests are not infrequent. Make several counts at each colony, preferably from different viewpoints to reach the correct total. If possible more than one visit should be arranged to ensure that late nesters are not omitted.

A good area to cover on this, or indeed any other local survey, is your own parish, the boundaries of which are marked on the 1:50,000 (approximately one and a quarter inches to the mile) Ordnance Survey map. An alternative and equally convenient area to cover is the ten kilometre square in which you live. This is the six-mile square boldly marked on the Ordnance Survey map, and for which a separate 1:25,000 (approximately two and a half inches to the mile) sheet is available. Each square has its own number preceded by two letters, such as SM90. Start to explore such an area and you may well be pleasantly surprised at the habitats and birds you have previously overlooked.

Another species which need not present too many problems to an observer wishing to engage upon a local survey is the House Martin. It is a familiar bird, often extending into city centres, and its nests are easily located beneath house eaves. Some still nest in ancestral sites on sea cliffs and occasionally quarries, though more care will be needed to locate these. In some areas river bridges are favoured and surprisingly large numbers may nest beneath these. The rate at which the House Martin colonizes new building estates is of interest. Not quite

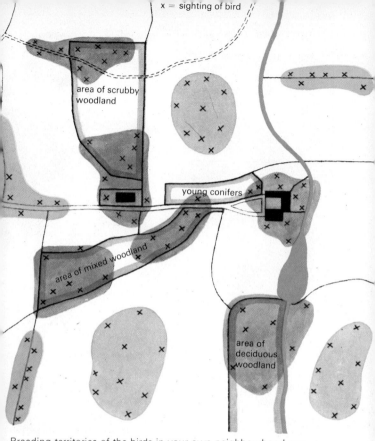

x = sighting of bird

area of scrubby woodland

young conifers

area of mixed woodland

area of deciduous woodland

Breeding territories of the birds in your own neighbourhood can be plotted on a large-scale map. This example shows territories of Blackbirds (pink), Yellowhammers (yellow) and Skylarks (blue).

so easy is the Sand Martin, making its main nest sites in holes in river and lakeside banks, sandpits and even railway cuttings and sand-dunes. The location of all colonies in your area, and annual visits to check on their fortunes, should prove a rewarding piece of fieldwork.

To try to survey all the bird species breeding in an area is not quite as impossible as it sounds, though to locate nests would be a full-time task. However, a good assessment of the population may be obtained by locating singing males during

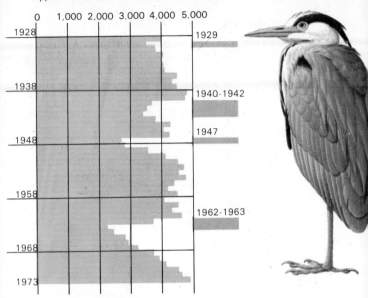

Approximate numbers of occupied Herons' nests

Heron populations are severely reduced in hard winters (blue bands). Results of the BTO census reveal how quickly the bird recovers from these setbacks.

the breeding season. An area suitable for this type of survey should not be too large, say about 200 acres (80 hectares), and one which the observer can expect to cover at least twelve times during the breeding season. The position of singing males is plotted on a large scale map (usually the twenty-five inch map), and when observations for several visits are combined the breeding territories are revealed. These may be confirmed by additional observations such as birds carrying nest material or food, or newly fledged young. These techniques were developed in Britain by the British Trust for Ornithology when they launched their 'Common Bird Census' in 1962. Several hundred observers now take part in this important survey, covering the same area with roughly the same effort each year, while new participants are always welcome.

The main aim of the 'Common Bird Census' has been to establish an index of the population of common British breeding birds, so that any changes can be noted and assessed.

This it has successfully achieved so that it is now possible to see the extent of changes in certain species. Some have declined, such as the Lapwing, Grey Partridge and Jackdaw. Others, such as the Wren and Mistle Thrush, have successfully recovered from the hard winters of the early 1960s. The Coal Tit, Goldcrest and Redpoll *Acanthis flammea* have each increased while, in addition to the Whitethroat among summer visitors, the Redstart and Sedge Warbler have declined. From the information received it is also possible, in these days of rapid changes to our countryside, to see what effect these are likely to have on our bird populations, so that the survey is of great value to the conservationist.

Since its inception in 1930, the British Trust for Ornithology has been responsible for many censuses and co-operative studies. Some have been only for a single year; others are carried out annually, or at regular, usually ten-year, intervals. The longest running of all concerns the Grey Heron *Ardea cinerea* in England and Wales. This actually began in 1928 under the auspices of the journal *British Birds*, and is thus one of the best censused populations of any wild creature in the world. The survey has shown just how much the Grey Heron suffers during hard weather and how its recovery rate is generally rapid; in recent years it has been slower, thought to be due to contamination by toxic chemicals. Nevertheless, the 1973 total of 4,925 nests was higher than in any other year.

The largest breeding season survey to cover a whole group of birds was that carried out in 1969–70 by over 1,000 observers taking part in 'Operation Seafarer'. Organized by the Seabird Group, the aim was to locate and count all colonies of the twenty-four species of seabird currently breeding in Great Britain and Ireland, providing an important baseline by which future population changes can be monitored.

The 'National Wildfowl Counts' comprise a long-running winter survey organized by the Wildfowl Trust. Observers are allocated a stretch of water and count any ducks, geese or swans present on certain dates at monthly intervals from August until April. The November and January counts coincide with the 'International Wildfowl Counts' in which observers from all over Europe and parts of North Africa and the Middle East take part.

## Bird pellets

The pellet or casting of a bird is the undigested portion of food – usually hard materials such as bones, teeth, insect wing cases and legs, grain and seeds – which are regurgitated through the mouth. These items are mostly surrounded by softer items like fur, feathers and vegetable matter, and on occasions even paper and plastic. Although pellets are normally associated with birds of prey, owls and large carnivorous or omnivorous species like gulls and crows, it has been found that their manufacture is much more widespread, having been recorded in about sixty species in Great Britain, including the Dipper, Robin and Yellowhammer.

Some pellets have peculiarities of shape and texture which identify the species from which they came, but in general there is a good deal of overlap and their origin needs to be confirmed by direct observation. Small passerines (perching birds) will have to be watched closely if pellets are to be collected, while knowing something of the habits of other pellet producers will enable the location of good samples.

Among birds of prey, possibly the Kestrel has most inter-

Pellets of the Short-eared Owl (A), Little Owl (B) and Eagle (C). After teasing out, the contents of a typical pellet might include a Sparrow hind toe (1), skull (2), humerus (4) and lower spine (6), Skylark breast feathers (3), vole skull (5), beetle wing case (7) and fur fragments (8).

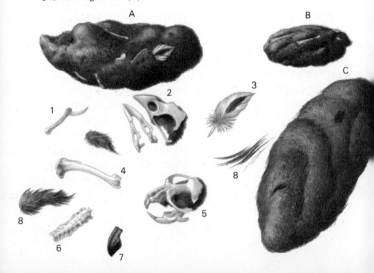

ested those studying bird diets. Its pellets are normally easy to find at winter roosts – on cliffs, quarries and ruined buildings – which are occupied continuously for several months. During the past few years analyses have been made of the food of this bird as determined by pellets from various parts of Britain.

Of all birds, the owls produce the best pellets; most prey is swallowed whole, and the intact bones easily resist their weak digestive systems. The Barn Owl uses a traditional roost for considerable periods, sometimes years, so that once located a regular supply of pellets may be collected. Those of the Tawny Owl are much more difficult to find in the gloom of the woodland floor, while the birds frequently move their roosting sites. A further hazard is that roosting high in trees means that many pellets disintegrate on branches or when they hit the ground. The Little Owl *Athene noctua*, an introduced species in Great Britain, aroused a great deal of controversy when it was accused as 'a wholesale destroyer of gamebirds, poultry chicks and songbirds'. An investigation in 1936–37 based partly on pellet material revealed that it fed mainly on insects and rodents; birds were generally taken only during the breeding season, with House Sparrow, Starling, Blackbird and Song Thrush the main species. Winter roosts are best examined for Long-eared Owl pellets, while the Short-eared Owl *Asio flammeus* ejects them regularly at vantage points within its hunting territory.

A representative collection of pellets is best mounted on white card in a clear container or insect store box; they attract pests such as mites so always include a pinch of naphthalene crystals. Of greater interest is the examination of pellets, particularly where batches can be obtained from the same roost. This can be a most rewarding exercise, yielding valuable information concerning the bird's diet. Pellets may be dissected dry using a needle and forceps, or may be soaked in water to separate the various items. Vertebrate skulls, even jaw bones and teeth, may be identified without difficulty, excellent keys for this being available in *The Handbook of British Mammals* edited by H. N. Southern, and the magazine *Bird Life* for April 1973. Bird remains are harder to identify although rings turn up from time to time and indicate the species taken.

## Caring for sick and injured birds

As birdwatchers we not infrequently encounter birds which, for a variety of reasons, cannot fly. Some are sick, but many will have been injured by collisions with telephone or electric cables, road traffic, or capture by the local cat. If we live near to the coast storm-driven and oiled seabirds will be the main casualties.

If you find a large number of dead or dying birds, *immediately inform* the Royal Society for the Protection of Birds. The most frequent cause of large scale mortalities is that of oil pollution affecting seabirds like the Guillemot. Occasionally poison or disease may be responsible so that the collection of specimens for later examination is essential. These should be stored in a deep freeze until arrangements can be made for their collection.

With a live bird the aim must *always* be the bird's rehabilitation and return to the wild in a healthy state at the earliest opportunity. Never look on your charge as a future pet. The Protection of Birds Act, 1954, stresses that the sole purpose of taking a sick or injured bird into your care is its release when no longer disabled. On the other hand the Act recognizes that the bird may survive but may be unable to fend for itself and so must remain in captivity.

When confronted with a sick or disabled bird try to assess how serious is its disability, at the same time considering whether you can provide all that is necessary for its recovery. In most cases this will require a good deal of time and patience, together with money spent on food and warm quarters. Birds with badly broken wings will rarely be able to fly properly again and will remain dependent on man. Bear such facts in mind before embarking on your rescue mission. If the bird is obviously beyond help then it must be humanely destroyed at once; a heavy blow on the back of the head is quick and merciful. Should you be unable to do this, take it to the nearest veterinary surgeon.

Should the bird seem to offer a chance of survival, but you are unable to provide the care and attention which it requires, do not pass on. There may be a 'bird hospital' in your locality; these have been established by volunteers in various parts of the country and are generally very good. The local inspector

Oil spills at sea usually result in seabird casualties, particularly among Guillemots.

of the Royal Society for the Prevention of Cruelty to Animals should be able to advise on this. Alternatively, a member of the nearest birdwatching society may care for the occasional bird in distress, although not operating on a 'bird hospital' scale. If such assistance is not available then the bird must be humanely destroyed to prevent further suffering.

Consult a veterinary surgeon if the bird is sick or has serious wounds or injury. It should always be kept warm and away from noise or sudden movement. A bird cage is ideal for small species; larger ones may require a garden shed or section of garage. Cover the floor with newspaper or cloth, *not* hay or straw which can lead to fatal lung diseases. Bread may be used as nourishment in the first instance, but recourse must be quickly made to natural foods. Do not forget water – birds like to drink and bathe, and the latter is a sign of recovery.

Young birds apparently abandoned should not be taken. The parents are probably close by and will return when you have gone. Should the youngster be in an exposed position, place it in the nearest cover. A check several hours later should reveal whether all is well. If it still seems in trouble, as a last resort you may take it home for feeding.

When you are sure a rehabilitated bird is ready for release, take it to the original point of discovery if possible, provided that it is the correct habitat for the species. Except for owls, release the bird early in the morning during fine weather so that they have the maximum time to feed and settle down before dusk. You may find it necessary to place food out for several days until the bird is fully able to fend for itself.

Sometimes you may come across freshly dead birds in good condition and these are often of great value to those museums with facilities for skinning and mounting, and who are always glad to receive specimens, even of the commonest birds. Certain species are required by the Monks Wood Experimental Station for research into contamination with toxic chemicals. These include all birds of prey (except the Buzzard), Great Crested Grebe, Heron, Kingfisher, Fulmar, Guillemot, Puffin *Fratercula arctica*, and most waders.

Dead birds which cannot be disposed of in these ways may still prove of interest. Why not make a collection of wings and feathers which can sometimes prove useful for reference. Wings should be removed by breaking the bone and cutting the tendons close to the body. The bare end of bone will have a little flesh adhering to it, and should be rubbed with powdered borax to prevent smell. Take both wings, setting one in an open position and retaining the other closed. When dry they are best mounted on stiff white card with details of their collection attached and then stored in a file box, or for large species, a drawer. Single feathers from known birds may be similarly mounted and stored.

Legs need to be cut off above the tarsus joint. A wire of suitable thickness is then inserted through the whole leg with a section protruding from the foot. This is pushed through stiff white card, bent forward and secured with tape. Sometimes bird footprints are found suitable for plaster of Paris casts. Wet sand, or better still firm silt or clay, provide good opportunities for preserving the footprints of shore birds.

Interesting collections can be made of shore bird footprints and feathers and wings taken from dead birds.

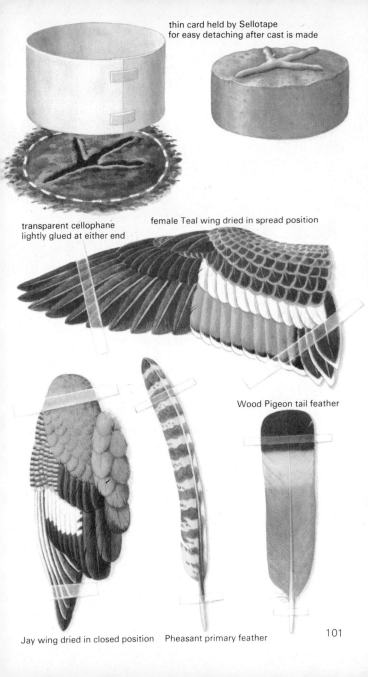

thin card held by Sellotape
for easy detaching after cast is made

transparent cellophane
lightly glued at either end

female Teal wing dried in spread position

Wood Pigeon tail feather

Jay wing dried in closed position     Pheasant primary feather

101

The location and size of Starling roosts can be established by plotting evening flight lines.

## Migration and local movements

Even at inland localities you may be surprised at the wealth of bird movement which takes place, particularly at migration time, but by no means restricted to it. The simplest form of bird movements are daily roosting and feeding flights. Who has not witnessed on late afternoons in winter small flocks of Starlings passing purposefully overhead, all travelling in the same direction? These are birds returning to roosts, usually in scrubby woodland and young plantations, or to buildings in urban areas. Roosts may be located by plotting the flight lines from observations at different points.

Among birds which make regular feeding flights in winter are gulls; many of the large reservoirs in lowland Britain, and several estuaries, provide them with safe roosting places. The main species involved in such movements are the Common *Larus canus* and Black-headed Gulls. Each morning the birds disperse from the roost, sometimes ranging to a radius of over 20 miles (32 kilometres) in search of food. The Common Gull, between August and March, for example, travels from the

River Severn on to the dry Cotswold uplands. Assessments of roost size may be obtained by watching the incoming flocks from the early afternoon onwards.

A good deal of diurnal migration is visible, particularly in autumn, even over the central areas of Great Britain. This is best observed during the hour or two after dawn from the tops of escarpments such as the Malvern Hills or East Anglian Heights. Flocks of Skylarks, thrushes, pipits and finches are the main birds to be seen, usually moving towards the south, affording as they do an opportunity of seeing migration in progress and the chance to record the species and numbers present.

During the 1960s it became apparent that large passages of seabirds can be seen from vantage points – headlands, even piers – virtually anywhere around our coast. At times birds move by at a considerable distance offshore so that identification to begin with can be difficult. The main species seen are Gannets, gulls, terns and auks, with smaller numbers of divers, Manx Shearwaters, sea ducks and skuas. There is always the chance of seeing something unusual like a Sooty Shearwater, Great Shearwater, Pomarine Skua *Stercorarius pomarinus* or Sabine's Gull *Larus sabinni*.

Seabird passage can be observed from vantage points such as headlands and piers.

Fulmar

Manx Shearwater

Sooty Shearwater

# Bird ringing

Never pass by a dead bird, however decayed, without first examining it to see if it has a small, light alloy ring on one or other leg. If it is ringed carefully make a note of the number and reference letter, together with the address. The ring can be returned, though this is not necessary providing that the correct number is sent. Never remove a ring from a live bird; once again carefully note the details before releasing it. Most likely the ring will be a British one, either having 'British Museum (Nat Hist), London, SW7' or 'B.T.O. Tring, England' as its address. Occasionally you may have the even greater excitement of finding a bird ringed abroad, perhaps a Lapwing from Denmark or a Starling from Russia. On reporting your discovery you will be informed of the species, locality and date of ringing, while the ringer will be given its recovery details.

A bird ring is open-ended, and when placed on the bird's leg it is carefully closed, sometimes using special pliers to ensure that it fits correctly. Some are overlapped and in others the ends are neatly butted, while their lightness ensures that the birds suffer no inconvenience. From time to time you may find rings that are solid, have only a number, and usually in association with a coloured rubber or plastic ring. These are used by racing pigeon enthusiasts, the rings being fitted at the chick stage by slipping them over the foot.

Bird ringing commenced at the beginning of this century and until 1937 two independent schemes were operated in Great Britain. These amalgamated in 1937 and are now controlled by the British Trust for Ornithology. At present about 500,000 birds are ringed annually in Great Britain, of which about 14,000 will eventually be recovered. The highest recovery rates are in large species, like gulls, because their bodies are more easily found, and among those which are regularly hunted, mainly ducks and geese. The chances of a small passerine being recovered are extremely small, less than one per cent, but data are nevertheless gradually being accumulated concerning movements, wintering and breeding ranges of the perching birds.

Ringing is a skilled art and a valuable tool, enabling us to learn much about the life histories of birds which could not otherwise be revealed. Some of the most striking recov-

Some examples of bird rings are shown and also the correct way to hold a bird for identification from the pattern of the wing feathers.

eries have been long distance ones like the two Arctic Terns found on the east coast of Australia, while others have reached Antarctica. A Pochard *Aythya ferina* once crossed Asia to the Sea of Okhotsk, and a Mallard penetrated the North American continent to Alberta, Canada. These are exceptional journeys; the main bulk of recoveries indicate the routes by which birds travel; where they spend the different seasons; even differences between age groups as in the Gannet, where young birds migrate to north-west African waters while the adults stay closer to the breeding colonies.

Many people wish to become ringers. First you must be a competent observer able to correctly identify birds, and then you must undergo long and careful training with a qualified person. The correct way to handle a wide variety of birds will be learnt; how to remove them from traps and nets; and how to ring and to keep records of the work. Only when this has been completed can a full ringing permit be applied for to the British Trust for Ornithology, together with a ringing licence from the Nature Conservancy Council.

# PHOTOGRAPHY

Many birdwatchers now naturally include a camera as part of their equipment, using it in the first instance for habitat pictures and general views. From this simple beginning, however, it is possible to progress through various stages, taking pictures of birds in all situations. Indeed, for some, this eventually becomes the mainspring of their hobby, just as bird ringing or sea watching may be for other observers. A 35 millimetre camera provides a negative or colour transparency size of 36 × 24 millimetres and is the type most widely used. There is a very wide range of cameras and equipment, and an excellent selection of colour film, to choose from. Some photographers prefer a larger size, $2\frac{1}{4}$ inches (5 centimetres) square, but the number of cameras available as well as the greater cost tend to put this beyond the reach of many people. You must not forget that an earlier generation of bird photographers did not have today's miniature cameras, and yet their work with plate cameras remains unsurpassed.

Although a new camera and accessories are to be preferred, costs may be prohibitive, and there is good secondhand equipment generally available. For this always seek the services and advice of a reputable dealer – the best always guarantees items sold. It also pays to shop around for the most competitive prices. These vary a good deal, even on the same model, and so a study of the photographic magazines and the nearest camera shops will ensure that the most suitable price is paid.

A single-lens reflex camera (SLR) is the most ideal type to purchase. A system of mirrors and shutters enables the subject to be viewed through the same lens which takes the photograph. Not only is accurate focusing ensured but the effect of parallax, which can lead to part of the subject being excluded, is ruled out. The camera should have a range of shutter speeds up to at least $\frac{1}{500}$ of a second, preferably to $\frac{1}{1000}$. Anyone wishing to progress to electronic flash and ultra-high speeds should ensure that the camera being purchased is properly synchronized for such work. Check that the shutter action is not too noisy; this is an important factor when working at close range from a hide.

Every film package contains an exposure guide, often with explanatory sketches. By following this, with care and a little

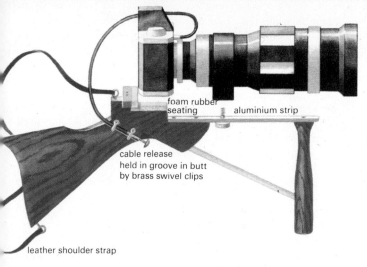

foam rubber
seating

aluminium strip

cable release
held in groove in butt
by brass swivel clips

leather shoulder strap

This 'rifle-butt' support is easily constructed and enables a camera
with telephoto lens fitted to be held steady.

experience, especially if the same film is always used it is
possible to make the right exposure without recourse to a
meter. This instrument is usually used, however, sometimes
incorporated into the camera and sometimes separately. It has
been said that 'the right exposure meter is a wonderful slave
but a bad master'. Certainly it is not simply a matter of blindly
following the meter reading; always be prepared to adapt to
the circumstances – perhaps a very bright subject, or one in
dense woodland – as necessary.

For taking bird photographs one further item of equipment
is required – the telephoto lens. As with binoculars special
care should be taken when purchasing, not forgetting that
cheap lenses usually turn out most expensive in the long run
for, rarely living up to expectation, they are replaced at an
early stage. The magnification of the telephoto lens may be
obtained by dividing its focal length by that of the camera lens
(the focal length is always engraved on the lens mounting).
For instance, a 500 millimetre telephoto lens associated with a
camera lens of 50 millimetres will have a magnification of
approximately ten times. The smaller the focal length and

magnification, the closer you will need to be to the subject so that a lens of 135 millimetres, though ideal for large, easily approached species such as certain seabirds, will not be at all suitable for distant and wary waders. A lens of about 300 millimetres is a good 'maid of all work', though for really long-range studies expensive 800 or 1,000 millimetres will prove necessary.

The weight and length of telephoto lenses mean that some form of support must be found for the camera. At a fixed point the familiar tripod with adjustable top is ideal, and when mobile in the field tree-trunks, gateposts, walls and even the car may be used as the opportunity occurs. Better still, employ a shoulder tripod in the form of a 'rifle-butt' support; several proprietary designs are available, though it is not too difficult a piece of equipment to construct. It needs hardly be added that it is essential for flight photography.

Hide construction has already been described (see pages 76–7). By using hides almost all bird species nesting in Europe have been photographed at the nest. Even so, a tremendous amount of photographic effort still concentrates on this aspect of a bird's life. When working at a nest the hide should be both built gradually and moved in stages towards the desired position, and removal should be equally cautious. Even when such precautions are taken a number of species are prone to

A strategically placed hide may be surrounded by large wader flocks at high tide, offering excellent opportunities for photography.

desert, so that extra care needs to be taken. It is perhaps better still to completely avoid these nervous species which include the Pheasant, Turtle Dove, Hawfinch *Coccothraustes coccothraustes* and Yellowhammer. Never use a hide at a nest where it will attract attention, and also ensure that your path to the hide and nest is kept as least trampled as possible. At the nest, however well screened, do not cut or remove vegetation, but rather tie it back with black cotton so that everything may eventually be replaced.

The other use of the hide is for what may be termed 'wait and see photography'. The hide is placed at a spot where birds are known to gather – a pool where they bathe, a feeding area, or for waders a high-tide 'roost'. For the sheer magnitude of numbers involved the latter is extremely exciting, and most of the classic wader photographs away from the nest have been taken by this means. The best-known site in Britain for wader flock photography is without question on the Hilbre Islands off West Kirby on the River Dee. As the tide rises birds feeding throughout this huge estuary, and numbering at times up to 150,000, are forced to certain spots where they gather until after high-water. The best point for seeing these is on Little Eye, smallest of the Hilbre Islands. A hide placed there is often surrounded by thousands of birds, at times pressing right up to its sides, so great are the numbers. The same technique may be applied to other estuaries, those without islands usually having a ridge or point where waders gather. Careful watching will soon reveal these, though a study of tide heights will also be necessary to ensure that the hide is not flooded and lives endangered.

Another means of attracting birds to a particular point for photography is by the use of food, the garden bird-table or feeding device being excellent for this purpose. The house may be the hide; alternatively the camera can be set up outside and operated by means of a remote control, long-distance shutter release. Special baits may be required for some species. Pheasants, for example, may be attracted by grain.

All photographers should have a copy of *The Nature Photographer's Code of Practice*, available from the Royal Society for the Protection of Birds on receipt of a first-class stamp.

Improvements in portable sound recording equipment have enabled many birdwatchers to record birds in the field.

## Sound recording

The recording of bird songs and calls has not as yet reached the scale of amateur bird photography, but is becoming more popular and provides valuable assistance with field identification. For this the recording need not have 'broadcasting' quality, and may include background noise, but it is still a far better method than trying to provide a verbal or written description of bird song. There is also no better way of learning bird song than by using your own recorder in the field, and then listening to the results at home. Tape recorders and their accessories are in fact cheaper than most photographic equipment, particularly if one is moving into the field of telephoto lenses or high speed work with electronic flash.

Developments during recent years mean that a variety of portable tape recorders is now available. Birdwatchers are gradually coming to accept these instruments as integral parts of their equipment, as much as binoculars and field guides. Powered by small batteries and equipped with sensitive microphones, the tape recorders of today are easy to operate.

Most use small cassettes of tape which provide up to 120 minutes of continuous recording. The reel-type recorder is better, however, because this allows straightforward cutting and editing of tape to produce a more satisfactory result.

An almost essential piece of equipment is the parabolic reflector – a shallow dish of metal or glass fibre, up to approximately 36 inches (90 centimetres) in diameter. The microphone is held by stays out from the centre and faces inwards. The reflector works on the principle that sounds striking its surface bounce back to the microphone, so increasing by as much as 80 times the level received. At the same time noises away from the bird tend to be excluded. Good parabolic reflectors can be expensive, but it is not too difficult to construct a substitute. The simplest form is no more than a cone of stiff cardboard and the old type of electric bowl fire has been found to be ideal, usually bought cheaply at old furniture sales or in secondhand shops. It is a straightforward task to remove the heating element and to substitute a microphone in its place.

Listen to any commercially made bird record and here and there can be heard background noises. Sometimes it is the sound of another bird, perhaps a distance cock Pheasant or a Cuckoo, a church clock striking or a cow lowing. These all add freshness to the record when in moderation. One background noise, however, is the arch-enemy of the sound recordist – the wind – and great efforts and not a little patience have to be employed in successfully combating this. Siting the microphone at low level is sometimes satisfactory, but by no means always convenient. A wind shield can be used and again can be 'home-made' requiring no more than a wire frame to enclose the microphone over which two layers of nylon stocking are stretched. Alternatively, a similar fine material may cover the whole parabolic reflector.

Even with a reflector you need to be in fairly close proximity to the bird, so that observation and careful planning are always needed. The microphone can then be set up close to the desired point, the tape recorder hidden close by and operated from a distance. With more expensive equipment, better operating conditions can be achieved by having microphone leads running several hundred feet from the recorder.

# INFORMATION FOR THE BIRDWATCHER

## Bird protection

The first Act to provide birds with protection in this country, other than for gamebirds, was passed in 1869 and covered seabirds. In the years which followed, other Acts came into force, some being of an extremely local nature, so that gradually the law concerning birds became so unwieldy as to be virtually unworkable. The situation was not clarifed until 1954 when the Protection of Birds Act was passed, followed by important amendments in 1967.

Basically, the present Act protects *all* wildbirds, their nests and eggs, although it allows certain exceptions for gamebirds and a few species considered pests. Thus, a Robin may not be shot or have its eggs taken, while a Common Snipe, classed as a gamebird, may be shot except between 1 February and 11 August. The Jackdaw, together with other injurious species, may be killed at any time, or have its eggs taken, but only by an *authorized person.* This is the owner or occupier of the land, or any person authorized by him, or someone authorized by the local authority or a body such as a river board.

For the birdwatcher the First Schedule is possibly the most important; this lists about seventy of the rarest species to nest in Great Britain. These receive special protection which makes it an offence to disturb them at the nest. Approaching the nest of these birds would constitute such an offence, and although most are rarely, if ever, likely to be encountered, there are some which could well be in your neighbourhood. These may include the Sparrowhawk *Accipter nisus,* Little Tern *Sterna albifrons,* Barn Owl, Kingfisher and Woodlark *Lullula arborea.*

Certain methods of killing or taking wildbirds are prohibited, irrespective of the species involved, and include baited boards, bird lime, hooks and line, tethered live birds as decoys, poison, snares, spring traps and stupefying baits.

From time to time birdwatchers encounter incidents which involve breaking the law. When this occurs take as many details as possible concerning the offence – the time it was committed, details of the offender's appearance, if a car was used, then the number. If you are accompanied, send someone

Unfortunately still set on some estates, the use of the particularly cruel pole trap is banned under the Protection of Birds Act, 1954.

for the police, otherwise do so yourself as soon as you have collected all the information you can. At the same time inform the nearest inspector of the Royal Society for the Prevention of Cruelty of Animals (listed in the telephone directory), and the headquarters of the Royal Society for the Protection of Birds. The latter have a useful booklet *Wild Birds and the Law* (sent on receipt of a first-class stamp).

Another important aspect of bird protection has been the provision of nature reserves. Some are immense, covering thousands of acres, while others are small like Grassholm, Pembrokeshire, a mere 22 acres (9 hectares). Most are owned or leased by national or regional organizations. The Nature Conservancy Council is a British Government body, established in 1949, concerned with nature conservation. Its reserves are varied and include important ornithological areas. Mention must be made of those at Hermaness, Shetland, and Scolt Head, Norfolk, with their seabirds, and Caerlaverock, Dumfries, and Lindisfarne, Northumberland, both premier sites for winter wildfowl.

The Royal Society for the Protection of Birds has over forty reserves in Britain. Some have been established with a particular species in mind, like Havergate Island, Suffolk, where Avocets nest, or Fetlar, Shetland, with its Snowy Owls *Nyctea scandiaca*. Others may have a much more general interest, like the recently acquired Nags Head, Gloucestershire, with a rich woodland avifauna. The National Trust also owns several ornithological sites, the most important being the Farne Islands, Northumberland. The county naturalists' trusts often have reserves of local ornithological interest and occasionally of national importance, like Needs Oar Point, Hampshire, with its tern colonies and immense gullery.

Another aspect of the Protection of Birds Act, 1954, is that the Secretary of State may establish sanctuaries. An outcome of this has been the system of wildfowl refuges, both of national importance, like the Humber Wildfowl Refuge, Humberside, or of regional importance, like Radipole Lake, Dorset. Shooting is prohibited or strictly controlled in these refuges and so they are virtually undisturbed.

Map to show European nature reserves and observatories.

■ National parks and nature reserves of ornithological interest

■ Bird observatories

## Bird observatories

During the last decades of the nineteenth century a German, Herman Gätke, founded an ornithological station on Heligoland, an island some thirty-five miles (fifty-six kilometres) north of the West German coast. Here he collected bird specimens, often encountered species and races previously unknown in western Europe, at the same time keeping records of the numbers and direction of the immense passage of commoner birds through the island. His classic work, translated into English in 1895 – *Heligoland as an Ornithological Observatory* – created great interest, and by 1910 the accent had moved from the collection of specimens to the large-scale trapping and ringing of birds. The observatory is still most active, with as many as 100,000 birds a day estimated passing at peak migration times.

One of a number of visitors to Heligoland in the 1930s was R. M. Lockley, at that time living on the island of Skokholm, Pembrokeshire. Fired with enthusiasm at what he saw he returned to his own island and constructed a trap, similar to that used on Heligoland. Now universally known as the Heligoland trap and a standard piece of equipment at all bird observatories, it is usually situated at a sheltered spot where migrants gather, for example, in a stream valley or garden. Constructed of wire netting, it may be up to 12 feet (4 metres) high and 60 feet (18 metres) across at the entrance, narrowing and twisting until the catching box is reached.

From his experience gained on Skokholm, R. M. Lockley together with W. B. Alexander, assisted members of the Midlothian Ornithological Club in 1934 with the erection of a Heligoland trap on the Isle of May, off Fife. So a chain of observatories commenced, to be interrupted by the war years, after which the initial two were joined by others extending from Fair Isle, Shetland, to St Agnes, Isles of Scilly, from Sandwich Bay, Kent, to Cape Clear, County Cork. Most are on small islands, but a few are sited on prominent mainland headlands. There is usually a resident warden and always simple but adequate accommodation for visitors. These spend

A Heligoland trap is basically a wire-netting funnel with a very broad mouth down which birds fly until they reach the catching box.

Fine mist netting is practically invisible to flying birds and is regularly used for trapping birds for ringing.

their holiday manning the traps and nets and learning the art of handling and ringing birds, and the operation of a bird observatory.

Migration is easier to study on the coast, hence the siting of observatories there. Islands have even greater advantages for this work, as once they have arrived birds are sometimes reluctant to move straight on, and so afford even greater opportunities for study. Small islands ensure that each part can be carefully worked daily, so that few birds are missed. A few observatories have a nearby lighthouse, the beam helping to attract migrants to the areas, sometimes with disastrous results, however. On Bardsey, Caernarvonshire, certain weather conditions result in several hundred birds killing themselves in a night by striking the tower.

Besides the Heligoland trap, an assortment of smaller devices have been used to catch birds, with at one time a great deal of effort being put into their design and use. Nowadays the accent is on the Japanese mist net, used in the Orient for hundreds of years to catch birds for the table, but introduced into Great Britain only in 1956. The nets are made of an especially fine black mesh and are usually about 20 feet (6 metres) in length, supported on poles 9 feet (3 metres) in length. Against a suitable background with a moderate or less wind they are virtually invisible. On colliding with the net, flying birds pocket themselves behind longitudinal, tightly stretched strings. Once caught the birds must be promptly removed for examination and ringing. The advantage of mist nets over the older traps is their mobility; they can be speedily erected at virtually any spot, and have thus greatly increased the numbers of birds trapped and ringed.

Although all observatories are concerned with migration, each has its own breeding season specialities and research work is usually undertaken on these. On Fair Isle, the Arctic Skua *Stercorarius parasiticus* colony has been studied for years, many birds now recognizable individually by being colour ringed. The Isle of May, with an expanding gull population, has been the site of several studies and experiments, while at Dungeness, Kent, observations are made on the Little Tern and other breeding birds of the shingle ridges. The Manx Shearwater has been studied on Skokholm for over forty years since R. M. Lockley first watched this bird on The Knoll, the hillock which shelters the observatory.

Even in midsummer then a holiday at a bird observatory can be a rewarding experience, but it is at migration time that the greatest excitement occurs. Everyone is up at dawn, visits being made to the Heligoland traps and other areas where migrants gather on arrival. Most will be common species, warblers, redstarts, flycatchers, or if in late autumn thrushes and finches, each resting or feeding before moving on. Amongst these, if one is lucky, will be a bird, or even birds, quite unknown – species that will require the use of notebooks, or if caught, examination in the laboratory, before identification can be made. Each year birds new to Great Britain are recorded at bird observatories, and occasionally new species to Europe.

## Ornithological societies

Most people on taking up birdwatching as a hobby soon find that they wish to become a member of an ornithological society. There are several national and numerous regional ones. The oldest is the British Ornithologists' Union (addresses on pages 122–23), founded in 1859 and best known for its quarterly journal *The Ibis*, which contains on a world basis papers on bird biology, behaviour and avifaunas.

In 1932 the British Trust for Ornithology was founded. This holds three national conferences annually, together with occasional regional ones, publishes the journal *Bird Study* and a most informative bi-monthly newsletter. The main work of the BTO centres around its co-operative enquiries. These provide members with the opportunity of putting something back into their hobby by assisting with surveys, at the same time not detracting from the pure enjoyment of watching birds. The BTO main office is at Tring, Hertfordshire, but every county has at least one regional representative, a voluntary post filled by a person having an intimate knowledge of local birds, and always willing to help and advise concerning them.

The Royal Society for the Protection of Birds has the largest membership of any conservation body in Britain. It administers over forty nature reserves, most of which are accessible to members, publishes the magazine *Birds*, and through its film shows and other publicity does a tremendous amount of work in bringing about a greater awareness of birds and their place in the present-day environment. For young people below the age of eighteen it runs the Young Ornithologists' Club, with its own magazine *Bird Life*. The YOC organizes weekly courses on birds during the holidays, often based at Youth Hostels in many parts of the country.

There are numerous local societies, mainly devoted to recording information about birds in their own areas. Most publish annual bird reports and frequent newsletters, arrange field meetings and lectures and are always pleased to welcome new members.

Some examples of the symbols used by bird protection societies in this country and abroad.

The Royal Society for the
Protection of Birds

Deutscher Bund für
Vogelschutz e.V.
(Germany)

Ligue Française pour la
Protection des Oiseaux
(France)

Stazione Romana per
L'Osservazione e la
Protezione degli Uccelli
(Italy)

British Trust for
Ornithology

Fondo d'Intervento per i
Rapaci (Italy)

# USEFUL ADDRESSES

*Bird observatories.* enquire at British Trust for Ornithology

*British Ornithologists' Union,* c/o The Zoological Society of London, Regent's Park, London, NW1 4RY

*British Trust for Ornithology,* Beech Grove, Tring, Hertfordshire

*Forestry Commission,* 25 Saville Row, London, W1X 2AY (Publishes booklets of ornithological interest; has nestboxes and arranges nature trails in many of its woodlands.)

*Monks Wood Experimental Station,* Abbots Ripton, Huntingdon

*Nature Conservancy Council,* 19 Belgrave Square, London, SW1
   *Headquarters for Scotland,* 12 Hope Terrace, Edinburgh
   *Headquarters for Wales,* Penrhos Road, Bangor, Caernarvonshire
   In England there are regional offices for:
      *the North,* Merlewood Research Station, Grange-over-Sands, Lancashire
      *East Anglia,* 60 Bracondale, Norwich, NOR 58B
      *the South-east,* Zealds, Church Street, Wye, Ashford, Kent
      *the South,* Oak Cottage, Hyde Lane, Brimpton, Reading
      *the South-west,* Roughmoor, Bishops Hull, Taunton
      *the Midlands,* Attingham Park, Shrewsbury
   (Information concerning nature reserves open to the public may be obtained on request from the appropriate office.)

*Royal Society for the Protection of Birds,* The Lodge, Sandy, Bedfordshire, SG19 2DL
   Has regional offices for:
      *Scotland,* 17 Regent Terrace, Edinburgh, EH7 5BN
      *Northern Ireland,* 58 High Street, Newtonards, County Down, BT23 3HZ
      *Wales,* 18 High Street, Newtown, Montgomeryshire, SY16 1AA
      *North of England,* 'A' Floor, Milburn House, Newcastle upon Tyne, NE1 1LE

*Seabird Group,* c/o RSPB, The Lodge, Sandy, Bedfordshire, SG19 2DL. (For seabird enthusiasts it publishes occasional newsletters and a most informative annual report.)

*Wildfowl Trust,* Slimbridge, Gloucestershire (Now has collections of waterfowl in several other parts of the country.)

*Young Ornithologists' Club,* The Lodge, Sandy, Bedfordshire, SG19 2DL

Local organizations are too numerous to list (no area is without one) but mention must be made of:

*Irish Wildbird Conservancy,* c/o Royal Irish Academy, 19 Dawson Street, Dublin 2 (Covering the whole of Ireland this has a number of important nature reserves, while its branches arrange many members' activities.)

*Scottish Ornithologists' Club,* 21 Regent Terrace, Edinburgh, EH7 5BN (Publishes a quarterly journal *Scottish Birds,* and arranges a full programme of lectures and field meetings through its branches in many parts of Scotland.)

For information concerning the nearest ornithological society in England and Wales, the reader is advised to write to the *Council for Nature,* c/o The Zoological Society of London, Regent's Park, London, NW1 4RY

All counties are also covered by a Naturalists' Trust which administers nature reserves, holds meetings and occasional field trips. Although dealing with the whole field of nature conservation, the ornithologist will find membership of the local Trust of great value. Its address may be obtained from the *Society for the Promotion of Nature Reserves* (SPNR), The Green, Nettleham, Lincoln.

When writing to any of these organizations, please include a stamped, self-addressed envelope.

# BOOKS TO READ

There is a tremendous wealth of bird books available at the present time; the small selection listed are currently in print and available at bookshops or on loan from public libraries.

*A Guide to the Birds of Wales* by David Saunders. Constable, London, 1974

*Birds of the British Isles* (12 vols) by D. A. Bannerman. Oliver and Boyd, Edinburgh, 1953–63

*Birds of the British Isles and their Eggs* by T. A. Coward. Warne, London, 1969

*Breeding Birds of Britain and Ireland* by John Parslow. Poyser, Berkhamstead, 1973

*Ducks, Geese and Swans* by Oscar Merne. Hamlyn, London, 1974

*Field Guide to the Birds of Britain and Europe* by Roger Peterson, Guy Mountfort and P. A. D. Hollom. Collins, London, 1974

*Field Guide to Birds' Nests* by Bruce Campbell and James Ferguson-Lees. Constable, London, 1972

*Finches* by Ian Newton. Collins, London, 1973

*Hamlyn Guide to the Birds of Britain and Europe* by B. Bruun and Arthur Singer. Hamlyn, London, 1970

*Popular Handbook of British Birds* by P. A. D. Hollom. Witherby, London, 1968

*Seabirds* by David Saunders. Hamlyn, London, 1972

*Seabirds of Britain and Ireland* by Stanley Cramp, W. R. P. Bourne and David Saunders. Collins, London, 1974

*Swifts in a Tower* by David Lack. Chapman and Hall, London, 1973

*The Herring Gull's World* by Niko Tinbergen. Collins, London, 1971

*The Life of a Robin* by David Lack. Fontana, London, 1965

*The Migrations of Birds* by Jean Dorst. Heinemann, London, 1962

*The New Bird Table Book* by Tony Soper and Robert Gillmor. David and Charles, Newton Abbot, 1973

*The Shell Bird Book* by James Fisher. Ebury Press, London, 1973

*Where to Watch Birds* by John Gooders. Andre Deutsch, London, 1967

*Woodland Birds* by Eric Simms. Collins, London, 1971

# INDEX

Page numbers in **bold** type
refer to illustrations

# SOME OTHER TITLES IN THIS SERIES

**Arts**
Antique Furniture/Architecture/Art Nouveau for Collectors/Clocks and Watches/Glass for Collectors/Jewellery/Musical Instruments/Porcelain/Pottery/Silver for Collectors/Victoriana

**Domestic Animals and Pets**
Budgerigars/Cats/Dog Care/Dogs/Horses and Ponies/Pet Birds/Pets for Children/Tropical Freshwater Aquaria/Tropical Marine Aquaria

**Domestic Science**
Flower Arranging

**Gardening**
Chrysanthemums/Garden Flowers/Garden Shrubs/House Plants/Plants for Small Gardens/Roses

**General Information**
Aircraft/Arms and Armour/Coins and Medals/Espionage/Flags/Fortune Telling/Freshwater Fishing/Guns/Military Uniforms/Motor Boats and Boating/National Costumes of the world/Orders and Decorations/Rockets and Missiles/Sailing/Sailing Ships and Sailing Craft/Sea Fishing/Trains/Veteran and Vintage Cars/Warships

**History and Mythology**
Age of Shakespeare/Archaeology/Discovery of: Africa/The American West/Australia/Japan/North America/South America/Great Land Battles/Great Naval Battles/Myths and Legends of: Africa/Ancient Egypt/Ancient Greece/Ancient Rome/India/The South Seas/Witchcraft and Black Magic

**Natural History**
The Animal Kingdom/Animals of Australia and New Zealand/Animals of Southern Asia/Bird Behaviour/Birds of Prey/Butterflies/Evolution of Life/Fishes of the world/Fossil Man/A Guide to the Seashore/Life in the Sea/Mammals of the world/Monkeys and Apes/Natural History Collecting/The Plant Kingdom/Prehistoric Animals/Seabirds/Seashells/Snakes of the world/Trees of the world/Tropical Birds/Wild Cats

**Popular Science**
Astronomy/Atomic Energy/Chemistry/Computers at Work/The Earth/Electricity/Electronics/Exploring the Planets/Heredity/The Human Body/Mathematics/Microscopes and Microscopic Life/Physics/Psychology/Undersea Exploration/The Weather Guide